BIBLE STORIES
THAT SPEAK
TO OUR HEART

BIBLE STORIES THAT SPEAK TO OUR HEART

Charles M. Wible

Paulist Press
New York/Mahwah, N.J.

Cover design by Sharyn Banks
Book design by Lynn Else

Library of Congress Cataloging-in-Publication Data

Wible, Charles M.
    Bible stories that speak to our heart / Charles M. Wible.
        p. cm.
    Includes bibliographical references.
    ISBN 0-8091-4214-7 (alk. paper)
    1. Bible stories, English. 2. Love—Biblical teaching. 3. Friendship—Biblical teaching. I. Title.
    BS551.3 .W53 2004
    220.9'505—dc22

                                                                2003016453

Published by Paulist Press
997 Macarthur Boulevard
Mahwah, New Jersey 07430

www.paulistpress.com

Printed and bound in the
United States of America

Contents

CONTENTS

I dedicate this book to my Mom and Dad,
whose love for each other and for me
first showed me the love of God.

Acknowledgments

I want to acknowledge and thank the many people who have had a hand in this work. To George Rich, fellow teacher, who first proposed the idea for a class on love stories in the Bible that gave me the notion of writing this book, I owe a debt of gratitude. I also have deep thanks for the libraries and librarians of St. Anthony-on-Hudson, Rennsalear, New York, and the Washington Theological Union, Takoma Park, Maryland, for their assistance in research. I have great appreciation for the hospitality of the Benedictine Monks of Mount Saviour Monastery, Pine City, New York, where I first had the quiet and the atmosphere to put pen to paper. I would also like to thank Mr. Anthony Tamberino and Fr. Melvin Blanchette, S.S. for their invaluable insights into the manuscript, and their encouragement to seek publication. Without the help and support of these people and these institutions, *Bible Stories That Speak to Our Heart* would have remained a dream.

Introduction

Have you ever been in love? Have you ever felt that feeling deep, deep inside you that combines elation, butterflies, strength, and weakness all at the same time? Have you watched the light shine out of the eyes of your beloved, and known that it shines just for you? Love is powerful. It moves people and nations; starts and ends wars; turns rulers into beggars; and gives riches to the poorest of the poor. Once we know love, however brief, it cannot be taken away from us.

I remember my first "love" as a teenager. It moved me to write songs and poetry. It gave me courage, even in my self-doubt, to ask the question, "Do you feel the same way?" And even though it was an immature love, and was not lasting, it changed me and left me better than I was before the experience.

I know the love of my best friends. It involves acceptance and support. Friendship is willing to give and take. It is the ability to just be myself and know that I will not be judged, or if so, not rejected because I act or believe differently. Some friendships come and go, while others, those special few of intimate love, stand the test of time and distance. These friends and their love help define me. They are my strength, and they say something good about me.

Love has touched my life. These relationships have moved me down the road of life in directions I would never have traveled alone. Some of these directions were dead ends.

Often there were choices to make. Which way should I turn? Which side street shall I explore? A decision for one path necessarily negates another, and may involve leaving a love behind or even ending a relationship. Always there is a change involved in such decisions. I make healthy choices and I make unhealthy ones, as do those I love. The decisions made in love help us to grow, while those made without love cause us to die a little. Since love has touched my life, I have never been the same.

Love is one of the most powerful of human emotions. Love is also a profound religious experience. We all know something of love through our families, our spouses, and our friends. Often it is in and through these relationships that we first come to know about God. Yet we also live in a world where love can seem to be disturbingly absent. Is God absent in these times, too? Many define love by what they see and hear on television, in movies, and through music. Often these media trivialize love and relationships. Love is turned into romance, and romance is fleeting. Where, then, can faith-filled people turn to learn about love? How about looking in the Bible?

We know that the Bible contains truth for our lives, but sometimes we need help in breaking open that truth, and some way of placing these age-old stories into the perspective of our contemporary lives. What, then, can the Bible tell us about human love, relationships, and God? The Scriptures are the self-revelation of God and hence are our source and archetype for defining love from the Judeo-Christian perspective. In fact, the history of this revelation—salvation history—can be seen as one continuing love story.

We begin with creation, and specifically with the creation of man and woman. What does the Bible tells us about God's intentions for humanity and their fruitfulness? How can we reclaim that intention in our own day? This book challenges the reader to see the goodness of human love as it reflects divine love. From here, we proceed through both the Hebrew and the Christian Scriptures searching for stories. The tale of Jacob, his wives, and his children gives us a negative view of family love, but still we see how God can bring healing. Ruth and Boaz show us that people of substance find each other even through adversity. Through David and Jonathan, we see the love of friends shaping their lives and destinies. The prophet Hosea examines the problem of infidelity and faithfulness. In the Book of Tobit, we see how faith in God can bring people together despite all obstacles. We explore the goodness of sexual love through the Song of Solomon.

Turning to the New Testament, we see in the righteous Joseph and the trusting Mary examples of love. Their choices and actions show that love is a deed as well as an emotion. Mary Magdalene reveals the growth of love from gratitude to commitment to proclamation as her experience of the Risen Lord helps her to find love even beyond the grave. The relationship between Jesus and Peter demonstrates the love that challenges us to become our better selves, while the enigmatic figure of the Beloved Disciple in the Gospel of John brings us back to the beginning. We are the "Beloved Disciple," and the way we show our love for Christ expresses itself in all our relationships.

So, we examine the Scriptures; we look for descriptions of love and the people and relationships who live out this love. As always, when we open the Bible with the eyes of faith we will see ourselves, too. In examining the lives and the loves of our ancestors in faith we will be examining our own experiences. We may find ourselves relating to the challenges, the heartaches, the joys, and the triumphs of love. In finding the meaning of these scriptural stories, we may possibly find the meaning of love in our own lives.

CHAPTER ONE

"God Is Love"

God is love, and those who abide in love abide in
God, and God abides in them. (1 John 4:16b)

Love is a faith experience. I cannot honestly say what kind of love I experienced first, the love of God, or the love of people, but I know that they are intimately entwined. My faith and experience of God is affected by the people in my life. I approach people in the way that I do because of my love and experience of God. To me, it is all part of the mystery of God, and the mystery of love.

Perhaps this is the idea that John is trying to portray in his letter. To understand God, we have to abide in love—but that love finds its source and fulfillment in God. It is not just the expression of God's nature, it *is* God's nature. God is love. Either this statement is nonsense, or it is the most startlingly profound statement ever made about divinity.[1]

What does all this mean? What does it tell us about falling in love? About being in love? Does love tell us about God? Or does God tell us about love? The answer to the preceding two questions is yes! I believe these are two sides to the coin of love. I believe that when we see human love, it reveals something about God, and when we experience God in our lives, it helps us to understand human love a little better. The First Letter of John is telling us about this truth. It is the lens through which we need to view John's description of love, as well as our own loving relationships. For where there is true love, we will find God, and where love is challenged, or broken, or false, we will find that God is absent. Either way, these experiences will tell us about God even as they tell us about ourselves.

Chapter Four of 1 John is our starting point. It is the most developed treatment of love in the New Testament. The verb *agapon* (to love) is used twenty eight times in 1 John, eighteen of which are contained in 1 John 4:7—5:4. Further, thirteen of the eighteen uses of *agapē* (love) are used in this same section.[2] Obviously, the author is making a point. It flows from his assertion that "God is love." This love encompasses, in John's mind, the whole of our lives as loving, faith-filled people. The sacred author says that our faith (what we believe in), and our ethics (what we do), are inseparable. This is why the commandment of love in 1 John 4:21–5:4 is placed in the context of our relationship with the Love-Who-Is-God. If we believe God is love, and we want to love God back, then we must love our brothers and sisters. Further, the extent to which we act out our love of brother or sister is identical with our love of God.

John goes on to say that our ability to love is itself a gift from God, whose love for us is primary. From it flows all other loving. Our response to God's love, however, is seen in the relationships we have with those around us. John declares:

> We love because he first loved us. Those who say, "I love God," and hate their brothers or sisters, are liars; for those who do not love a brother or sister whom they have seen, cannot love God whom they have not seen. The commandment we have from him is this: those who love God must love their brothers and sisters also. (1 John 4:19–21)

Thus, God's love for us, shown in the gift of Jesus, bids us to return that love by the way we love one another. Abiding in love, then, is put into practice when we show love for others.

Of course, this way of loving is an ideal. No one can love perfectly. Even at the best of times, my love of neighbor can be selfish. Even at my most spiritual moments, my love of God is clouded by doubt. Yet, these ideals are also practical. This love-of-God, love-of-neighbor parallel is the measuring stick of my life. At the end of the day I can say that I have seen God today in the moments that I have truly tried to love others, and I can resolve to grow in my love of God by my determination to be more loving tomorrow. I can learn about God, about myself, and about my brothers and sisters by examining my ability to love and be loved, and conversely, to hurt and be hurt.

In many ways, this concept is very human. Even outside the realm of faith, the ability to make and maintain loving relationships is a sign of a healthy psyche. And it is the emotional baggage which we carry from our failures to love or feel loved that is the material used by psychologists and counselors to help us work through our problems and integrate ourselves into whole and healthy persons.

The same is true of our love of God. Is it not our inability to love that we define as sin? So often it is our incapacity to love, or to be loved and feel lovable, that prevents us from letting God into our lives, or even believing that God exists. It is in the human experience of loving that the love of God is found. I am not saying that the love of God is merely a human activity, but that the human activity of love is often the gateway into the realm of God's love. Grace builds on nature, the saying goes, divine love builds on the foundation of human love. Yet, we must always remember that the source of human love is the creative power of God. God first made us to be loving beings because, as a loving being, that was the greatest gift God could give us. The sign of God's love for us is our ability to love one another. And when we love one another, do we not return God's love in a profound and beautiful way?

The loving of brother and sister, however, is a many faceted reality. Because we can experience love, or its absence, in a variety of ways and through a variety of people, love is far from simple. Again, if you have ever been in love, you know how complex it can be. It behooves us, then, to look at the many faces of human love and see what they can tell us about God and ourselves.

We do not have far to look. Besides the experiences of our own lives and relationships, there are archetypical stories that strike chords in our souls. Our own Scriptures contain so many that it is hard to narrow them down. I would like to choose a few, from both the Hebrew and Christian Testaments, which bring out some aspects of this love relationship. We will see in these scriptural stories both the presence and the absence of love. By examining these love stories, and the relationships that are told through them, we will see and learn something about what it means to say, "God is love," and what it means to believe "those who abide in love abide in God, and God abides in them." And in the telling of these stories, we will see and hear our own story so that we, too, can know how our love brings us into intimate contact with the God who first loved us, and whose love calls us into loving relationships with one another.

Reflection Questions

1. How have experiences of love and friendship helped you to find God in your life?
2. Who are the people whose love has had an impact on your life and why?
3. What does the author of 1 John mean by "abiding in love?"

Notes

1. Leon Morris. *Testaments of Love—A Study of Love in the Bible.* Grand Rapids: William B. Eerdmans Publishing Company, 1981, p. *x*.

2. Raymond E. Brown, S.S. *Epistles of John.* Anchor Bible. Garden City: Doubleday & Company, Inc., 1982, p. 546.

CHAPTER TWO

Adam and Eve

"This at last is bone of my bones and flesh of my flesh."

It does not take us long to find the first love story in the Bible. The stories of creation that are recounted in the beginning of the Book of Genesis begin a love story that is, as yet, unfinished. It is the story of God's love for us, for creation itself is a love story. God creates because God is love, and love must be fruitful; love must be creative. It is not by accident that God created "the heavens and the earth" (Gen 1:1), and everything that is in them. Unlike the creation myths of the surrounding cultures in the ancient Near East, the Hebrew stories of creation show that God had a plan and a purpose in creating the world, both of which were expressions of God's love. The Divine Initiative is an act of love that bears fruit in the making of the earth, the plants, and animals and, ultimately, in the creation formed "in our [God's] image, according to our likeness…" (Gen 1:26).

It is these creatures, the first humans, to which we now turn. Their story unfolds in the second chapter of Genesis; it is a story of power and beauty and danger. It is a tale of loneliness and fulfillment. It is a journey of discovery. The creative power of God moves slowly to completion, and it is not complete until the man and the woman stand naked but unashamed in each other's presence, at ease with themselves, with each other, and with God. Integrated in action and attitude, they are one in flesh and bone.

The so-called "Second Story of Creation," told in Genesis 2:4–25, is attributed to the Yahwist source,[1] a ninth century B.C. storyteller who used the oral traditions and origin stories of his people to teach about the existential situation of the Davidic times, in which these stories were written down. In other words, the Yahwist author wrote creation accounts not to record how we came to be, but to explain why we are the way we are. The story of creation in Genesis 2, therefore, explains the relationship between human beings and nature, as well as the power of the attraction between man and woman. This story is not only about the creation of humanity, but also about the creation of sexuality and why it is such a strong force in human life.

The Yahwist author is a consummate storyteller. Genesis 2 is filled with captivating images and subtle word plays. It shows an almost playful God, with sleeves rolled up, molding with clay, planting a garden, and sharing creative power with the human he had created.

The first play on words in the story has to do with the first act of creation. Out of the "dust of the ground" (in Hebrew, *hā'ādāmâh*), God creates the "earth creature" (*hā'ādām*). Adam is not meant to be a proper name here, but rather a descriptive title. "Adam" is the creature made from the earth. Adam is not identified as male, because gender and sexuality have not as yet been created.[2]

What makes this earth creature so special is that God "breathed into his [sic] nostrils the breath of life" (Gen 2:7). God fills this creature with breath, or *spirit*, and so *hā'ādām* becomes "a living being." It is the only time in the narrative that this action is described. *Hā'ādām* is made from the earth, and thus has affinity to it, but *hā'ādām* is also a living being filled with God's breath or spirit. *Hā'ādām* has affinity with God as well.

God then plants a garden for *hā'ādām*. It, too, is formed out of the earth, and *hā'ādām* is related to it. There is unity in creation; we are made of the same stuff. Yet, the relation of *hā'ādām* to the garden is special. Already God shares power with the earth-creature, who is to care for, literally "husband" the garden. While the Yahwist author knows that humanity and nature are often at odds with one another, he also knows that such was not the intention of the Creator. Sin, which is discussed in Genesis 3, has driven a wedge between the earth and the earth-creature, but this situation is a tragedy. It is a situation we are called and challenged to remedy if the love story of creation is to continue.

Hā'ādām is not given ultimate authority over the garden, however; there are limits. The story adds a note of moral responsibility as well. There are rules in this garden. The garden surrounds the Tree of Life (about which no prescriptions are given), and the Tree of Knowledge (whose fruit is forbidden). The Tree of Knowledge does not symbolize omniscience, nor moral choice, though both these elements are present in the prohibition. The phrase "knowledge of good and evil" is a Hebrew figure of speech that connotes "and everything in between." To possess such knowledge implies moral judgment. This is not to say, however, that *hā'ādām* does not know right from wrong until after the forbidden fruit is eaten. If *hā'ādām* did not know right from wrong, then the command not to eat from the Tree of Knowledge would be incomprehensible.

The Tree of Knowledge symbolizes limitation. *Hā'ādām* shares in God's creative power. This power is a gift—the gift of being a "living being." The earth-creature is to husband the earth. Later that care will be extended to the animal world as well. The earth-creature, however, is not God's equal. The knowledge, power, and prerogatives proper to divinity are protected and prohibited. There are some things that human beings just cannot know, and just cannot do. While it is our nature to strive to better ourselves, we also need to accept our limitations, and maintain the proper relationship between the divine, the human, and the natural orders. Harmony exists in creation when creature and Creator recognize and accept their respective roles. The Tree of Knowledge represents a knowledge that is beyond the ken of a creature, and so it is forbidden. The tragedy of Genesis 3, the tragedy of human life and sin, is our constant rejection of our role as creature. The Yahwist author knew this; it was evident in the trials and tribulations of his day. We know this, too. It is what causes so much pain in our relationships with each other and with the world around us, but this brokenness is not the intention of the Creator.

The loving story of creation continues as God comments about *hā'ādām*'s aloneness. Here, for the first time, God says, "It is not good" (Gen 2:18). The creative process continues in answer to this need. Again out of the earth, God forms the birds of the air and the beasts of the field. God brings these animals to the earth-creature to be named. God shares creative power with *hā'ādām* once more. In the ancient world, to name something was to exercise control over it. As the earth-creature names each animal, he takes responsibility for it, similar to the responsibility he has over the garden. But responsibility is not companionship. Out of all the creatures God has made, no suitable partner is found. Nothing has been made with which *hā'ādām* can share on a personal level. The other creatures, though made from the same earth, are not "living beings," in the way that *hā'ādām* is. For into none of the other creatures did God breathe the life-giving spirit. They are unable, therefore, to be suitable partners for *hā'ādām*; they are not equals.

So the story now moves from straightforward creation narrative into the realm of mystery. The earth-creature falls into a deep sleep. Sleep in the Bible is often a symbol of penetrating and mysterious happenings. Sleep is that place between life and death where visions happen, angels congregate, and God moves unseen. It is in this time of deep sleep that God does something different. For the first time in this story the stuff of creation is not the earth, not *hā'ādāmâh*. To make a suitable partner for *hā'ādām*, God makes something *out of hā'ādām*.

God removes one of the man's ribs, and out of it, God forms the woman. For the first time in this story these words, man and woman, are proper. What God creates here is gender and sexuality. Gender, the difference between male and female, and sexuality, their ability to relate to one another as man and woman, are the capstones of the creative process. In both the creation stories of Genesis 1 and 2, the words "male and female" are applied only to humanity. While the animals are told to be fertile and multiply (Gen 1:22), only when humans are created does the text ascribe sexual differentiation to them (Gen 1:27).[3]

That the woman is made from the rib of the man has often been misunderstood to denote subordination of the female to the male. This situation was indeed the experience of the Yahwist author in ninth-century patriarchal society. Yet we must remember the agenda of the Yahwist source. He is not trying to justify, rationalize, or support the existential situation; rather, he is trying to criticize it. The sacred author is certainly aware of the sharp inequalities between the sexes, and in many ways, as a product of ninth century B.C. he accepts them. The Yahwist source is not suggesting a revolution in the gender roles of his day. He is aware, however, that the relationship between man and woman, between humanity and nature, and between nature and God has been broken. He is aware that God intended for all creation to live in harmony and that the current state of the world is the result of Sin, but in describing the original harmony of creation, especially in this scene of the creation of sexuality, the Yahwist author is anything but sexist in his view. His presentation is aimed at portraying unity, not division. The whole purpose of using the rib of *ha'ādām* was to make a suitable *partner*—a creature that corresponded to the man. The rib symbolizes this correspondence, and it stands for equality. Some writers have posited that *rib* is a Hebrew wordplay, noting that in ancient Sumerian *rib* and *life* were similar words. The image here, then, would be that man and woman are the very *life* of each other.[4]

This correspondence and equality between the man and the woman is further emphasized by the man's reaction when he meets the woman for the first time. Significantly, we hear the man's voice for the first time, as if to say, "only now is this earth-creature complete so that he speaks with his own voice what his heart tells him." The words he speaks are significant, too:

> "This at last is bone of my bones and flesh of my flesh;
> this one shall be called Woman, for out of Man this one
> was taken." (Gen 2:23)

The man's first words break forth in song—in poetry—the language of love. The declaration of woman as his bone and flesh has several interpretations. The simplest of which is the way we still use this phrase. To say "my flesh and bone" is to recognize kinship. If the earth-creature has affinity to the earth because it is the stuff of which he is made, then how much more so does he recognize his connection with the woman. The relationship between man and woman is more powerful than any other relationship in the created order because they are, indeed, made of the very same stuff. This woman is the suitable partner, the creature corresponding to him.

Further, in Hebrew idiom the word *flesh* denoted weakness (not the moral weakness of later NT writings) because it was soft. *Bone*, conversely, meant strength because it was hard. As we have seen, to name two extremes in Hebrew wordplay has the connotation of "and everything in between." Therefore, in calling the woman "bone of my bone and flesh of my flesh," the man is recognizing the woman as his other self. He is acknowledging the completeness of creation in the complementarity of the sexes. In weakness and in strength they are the same, and thereby have the ability to support one another. When man is weak, he draws from the woman's strength, and vice versa.[5]

Moreover, this phrase "bone of my bone and flesh of my flesh" is seen elsewhere in the Scriptures. Sometimes translated as "flesh and blood," the Hebrew terms "flesh and bones," can mean close relationship. In Genesis 29:14, Judges 9:2, 2 Samuel 5:1, 2 Samuel 19:13–14, this phrase may also be an example of an early covenant formula. It is part of an oath that promises fidelity in frailty and power, in good and bad times.[6] In this sense, the poem which the man speaks amounts to a marriage ceremony, and the man and the woman enter into covenant with one another.

Covenant is a very important idea in the Scriptures. It denotes more than a contract or agreement. While the concept finds its source in the Suzerainty treaties of the Ancient Near East, where a powerful ruler makes a pact with a vassal, in scriptural terms the word *covenant* very quickly takes on spiritual overtones. Unlike an agreement or contract based on law, a covenant is based on love. It implies total giving, with nothing held back. Covenant presumes trust and trustworthiness. These images, contained in such a small word, have framed our marital imagery throughout the centuries. Indeed this is the language of sacrament, and for the Yahwist writer, it explains the power of the relationship between husband and wife.

The man's poem about the woman continues with another Hebrew play on words:

> ...this one shall be called Woman, for out of Man this one was taken. (Gen 2:23)

In Hebrew, as in English, the word for man *(ish)* and the word for woman *(ishah)* are related. At first glance, however, it seems that the man is naming the woman, just as he did the animals. If this were so, then *hā'ādām* is once again asserting his control over the woman and the inequality of the sexes is once again maintained. Such is not the case. If any naming is going on here at all, the man is naming himself in relation to the woman. For the first time, gender-specific terms are used in this chapter, as if to say that the man recognizes himself for who he is only when he sees the woman. *Ish* and *isha* are mirror images of each other. The cleverness of the play on words is that both express the same reality, while at the same time pointing out the difference between the two. The mystery and wonder of the Creator here is that in dividing *hā'ādām* into male and female, in creating sexual differentiation, God has completed the human person. This difference and similarity make possible the substance of man and woman coming together as "one flesh" (Gen 2:24). This unity is experienced in the marital relationship even despite the brokenness of human relations and the inequality of the sexes that the Yahwist source experienced in his own time. It is what has made the marriages of men and women down through the ages rise above the narrow-mindedness of male-dominated society. It is also what makes the failure of marriages such a painful experience. Knowing the possibility of the unity that man and woman can achieve, experiencing glimpses of it in their own attempts at marriage can serve only to make the disappointment of failed relationships that much more stark and destructive.

And yet, when it does work, when man and woman come together and find in each other their destined equality and mutuality, are not the presence of God and the blessings of creation felt in an intimate way? Is this not how man and woman, in the first blush of creation, could stand naked in each other's presence, and naked before God, and feel no shame? Because they were made for each other, and found in each other completeness and love, the man and the woman are fully satisfied with who and what they are. In this acceptance of self and other, they are able to be themselves in the face of God. The picture that the Yahwist source paints is one of harmony in the created order: God, the Creator; humanity, God's image and likeness; and nature itself, for whom the man and the woman share the cocreative responsibility of caretaking, and which provides sustenance and beauty for the woman and the man. This triad, God-humanity-nature, provides balance, happiness, and peace. It is the way God intended for creation to be.

Now, we know, as did the Yahwist writer, that this balance and harmony do not exist. The coming of sin, described in Genesis 3, breaks this harmony, and humanity's relationship with God, with nature, and within itself suffers almost irreparably from it. We no longer stand before God and each other without shame. And yet...and yet, there is something in our human experience of the relationship between man and woman that makes this story of Genesis 2 resonate in our souls. Countless men and women down the centuries have found in each other the truth of this original harmony of creation. They see in each other "bone of my bone and flesh of my flesh," and recognize their mutuality. In the sexual attraction of one for another, they find a connection that goes beyond sex and creates intimacy. In the midst of the conflicts and problems of human relationships—the lack of communication, the frustration that comes when two individuals come together—two do become one. They find love.

Because they are suitable partners, companions, covenant lovers, then man and woman are able to trust, to grow, and to be creative in and for each other. They find God. For when one is vulnerable enough to open up to the possibility of love and covenant commitment, when man and woman learn to give and receive love, and recognize in each other their complete self, then they are ready to see, in each other, the face of God whose image they are.

Reflection Questions

1. What does it mean to be part of the "good creation" in the face of so much that is broken and tragic in our world?
2. How can we express our affinity with God in our relationships, our care for the environment, and our spirituality?
3. What does it mean for man and woman to be "flesh of flesh, and bone of bone?" How can our Christian relationships work toward restoring the original harmony that God intended for humanity?

Notes

1. For more information on sources and authorship in the Pentateuch, see Roland E. Murphy, O.Carm., "Introduction to the Pentateuch," *The New Jerome Biblical Commentary*. Eds. Raymond E. Brown, S.S., Joseph A. Fitzmyer, S.J., and Roland E. Murphy, O.Carm., Englewood Cliffs, N.J.: Prentice Hall, Inc., 1990, pp. 4–5.
2. Phyllis Trible. *God and the Rhetoric of Sexuality*. Overtures to Biblical Theology, Eds. Walter Brueggeman

and John R. Donahue. Philadelphia: Fortress Press, 1978, pp. 84–86; Raymond Collins, "The Bible and Sexuality," *Biblical Theology Bulletin.* VII (Oct., 1977) 4, pp. 153–154.
3. Trible, pp. 79–80.
4. Bruce Vawter. *A Path Through Genesis.* New York: Sheed & Ward, 1956, p. 75; Collins, pp. 154–155.
5. Walter Brueggemann, "Of the Same Flesh and Bone," *CBQ* 32:1970, pp. 534–535.
6. Brueggemann, *CBQ*, pp. 535–537.

CHAPTER THREE

Jacob, Rachel, and Leah

Jacob loved Rachel more than Leah.

From the hopeful and positive view of sexuality and marriage we examined in the story of Adam and Eve, it does not take long to find trouble. Adam and Eve's self-acceptance of their role in creation quickly falls to the sin of pride. In grasping after the prerogatives of God, symbolized by their partaking in the fruit of the Tree of Knowledge, the man and the woman are introduced to shame, disruption, and brokenness. They no longer see each other as equals, and the balance that existed between God, humanity, and nature is toppled. It is a sad story, but not without hope. Even in the midst of sin and punishment, salvation is promised (Gen 3:15).

The first sin is felt in the world, and the wedded bliss that might have been follows a rocky road. Sometimes we see less "abiding in love" in marriage than we would hope, and God can seem cruelly distant. Immaturity, infatuation, jealousy, and rivalry can be the characteristics that surface in our relationships. These attributes can prevent the harmony envisioned in the creation stories from taking hold, and cause serious damage to people's lives and loves. We can see this reality played out clearly in the story of Jacob starting in Genesis 25.

Jacob has often been called the father of the first "dysfunctional family." From the very womb Jacob fights with his twin brother Esau (Gen 25:22–26), and their relations with each other into early adulthood are anything but peaceful and loving. Each is the favorite of a different parent, Esau being preferred by Isaac, while Rebecca is partial to Jacob. Jacob shows himself to be unscrupulous, devious, and self-serving. He buys his brother's birthright (i.e., Esau's right to inherit the larger share of Isaac's estate), and conspires with his mother Rebecca to trick his aging, blind father into giving Jacob the blessing intended for Esau.

The spoken word had great impact in the times of the patriarchs. In a preliterate culture, the saying of a promise or blessing was more binding than many a written contract in our own day. Words had power. Once spoken, a word could not be called back, and so, even though accomplished by trickery, Jacob inherits the blessing that initiates him into the covenant God had made with Abraham and Isaac. Jacob, though younger, becomes the patriarch of the family, and the promises made to Abraham and renewed through Isaac will now flow through him.[1]

All of these episodes serve to indicate the kind of person Jacob is. We are left with the picture of a cunning and dishonest man who, having manipulated his way to prominence, now must flee the wrath of those he has cheated. Rebecca sends Jacob back to the land of her birth, where the saga of Jacob's lovelife begins in earnest.

When Jacob reaches Haran, the homeland of his mother, he goes immediately to the community well. This well was more than just a place where shepherds came to water their flocks and women came to draw water for their homes. It was also a community gathering place, the place where gossip was traded and news exchanged. It was a natural place for a stranger to come if he wanted to find his distant relatives.

Further, there is a biblical leitmotif at work here. In Scripture, a single man coming to a well almost always finds a wife. It was how Rebecca was found for Isaac (Gen 24:10–27), and how Moses met Zipporah—at the well of Midian (Exod 2:15–22). So now Jacob comes to the well at Haran and meets his future bride, Rachel. We could call the meeting of Jacob and Rachel "love at first sight." He is obviously enamored of Rachel, who is described as being very beautiful (Gen 29:17), and he asks for her hand at the very first opportunity. On the other hand, it is only after Jacob sees the size of Laban's (Rachel's father's) flocks, and the richness of Laban's dwelling, that he expresses his kinship and love for Rachel (Gen 29:9–19).

Jacob offers, quite generously, to work for his uncle for seven years in exchange for Rachel. As Jacob was most probably penniless at this point in his life, this time of labor would replace the "bride price" that a man or his family had to offer a father for the hand of his daughter. In the patriarchal society of the second millennium before Christ, a daughter represented property in much the same way as a slave, and her father was compensated for the loss of her work by the paying of a "bride price." That Jacob was willing to work for seven years was exorbitant, showing how much he was willing to sacrifice to obtain her. The Scriptures tell us that these years "seemed to him like a few days because he loved her so much" (Gen 29:20). We see Jacob in a softer, more flattering light in this passage. A certain romance is indicated in Jacob's labor of love. Ancient mores concerning relationships between men and women would have precluded Jacob's spending much time with Rachel, or being alone with her at all. This separation of years could have been torturous to Jacob, but he endured it joyfully, knowing the prize that awaited him at the end. Such is the power of love.

Alas, however, love does not seem even to be a motivating factor in Jacob's life and relationships. On the long-anticipated wedding night, the deceiver is himself deceived. Ancient custom, still practiced among the Bedouins of today, called for the bride to be heavily veiled.[2] Thus was Laban able to substitute Leah, Rachel's older, and seemingly less attractive, sister for the beloved bride. Once the morning light revealed the deception, it was too late, for the marriage had been consummated. Leah was Jacob's legal wife and the seven years of labor for Rachel now must have seemed empty and long.

Remember, Laban knows Jacob's story. Jacob came to Haran not to find a wife, but to flee the wrath of his brother Esau whose inheritance he had stolen. When asked why he had tricked Jacob, Laban's response is almost an insult. "In this country," he says, "we respect the rights of the eldest." In the face of such reasoning, Jacob can only acquiesce. He contracts for a further seven years for Rachel (he will not give up on his dream of love), and suddenly has two wives.

In the story that follows of Jacob, Rachel, Leah, and their children, love is hardly ever an influencing factor. The rivalry and competition between the two sisters almost makes the disagreements between Jacob and Esau pale by comparison. Leah is unloved by Jacob, so she tries to buy his affection through her children. Rachel sees the bearing of children, and consequently her initial barrenness, as a challenge to Jacob's love for her. Rachel falls back on the ancient custom of providing a concubine for Jacob, and then adopting the children born of this slave girl as her own. In itself, this is not an unusual custom from the ancient world; it is not, in itself, a competitive gesture. Yet, the way Rachel goes about it, and the names she gives to her "adopted" sons, confirm her competitive spirit.

That Leah gives her maidservant to Jacob and adopts the children of this union is more puzzling. She has already provided heirs for Jacob, and is under no obligation to produce more. Hence, the motivation behind giving the slave Zilpah to Jacob can only be seen as her entry into competition with Rachel.

The catalog of Jacob's sons' names is a showcase of this competition. The names of Leah's children show how she tries to gain Jacob's love through them. The names that Rachel gives to Bilhah's children (and eventually to her own) reveal how she constantly seeks to show up her sister. All in all, the naming of Jacob's sons indicates a selfishness on the part of their mothers that is almost in contradiction to the spirit of motherhood.

Leah begins the competition by bearing four sons in a row. The name of the oldest son, Reuben,[3] means "he has seen my affliction." Leah believes that God has given her a son so that Jacob will now love her, but such was not the case. Simeon, the name of the second of Leah's natural children means "he has heard," and is interpreted by Leah to mean that God is favoring her because of Jacob's neglect. The name of the third son, Levi, means "he will be united," and shows Leah's hope that there still might be some love for her from Jacob. Judah, whose name means "I will praise," is the one seeming exception to the naming competition, perhaps foreshadowing the prominence Judah will have in the history of the people of Israel.

Rachel, who has Jacob's love, still wants more. She is childless and unhappy. She berates Jacob for not giving her children, as if it is his fault. The Bible contains many examples of women who are seemingly barren. In all of these instances, the women (Sarah in Gen 21:1–9, Samson's unnamed mother in Judg 13:2–7, Hannah, the mother of Samuel, in 1 Sam 1:9–18) are aware that it is God who provides life and fertility, and they address their petitions to the Lord. Rachel demands from Jacob what he cannot give. In her desire, she turns bitter toward the husband who loved her regardless of whether she had children or not.

So Rachel takes matters into her own hands. She provides Jacob with her slave Bilhah, adopts the sons Bilhah bears to him and names them. First there is Dan, whose name means

"God has vindicated me," as if his birth gives Rachel a step up on her sister. Naphtali, the name of Jacob's second child by Bilhah, means "I have struggled greatly," raising the competition with Leah to the level of a wrestling match. The begetting of children here is not about joy; rather, it is about battles won and lost in an attempt to manufacture love and respect.

Leah now presents her maid, Zilpah, to Jacob, so that the competition may continue, and two more sons are born. The names Gad, meaning "what good luck," and Asher, meaning "happy am I," again betray the sentiment that this family is all about possessions. Leah feels she is fortunate and lucky, and hopefully more important because she has provided more sons for Jacob.

Next, Leah "buys" time with Jacob. She trades the mandrakes (thought to enhance fertility), that her son Reuben had picked, for Rachel's usual night with Jacob, and, as a result, gives birth to Issachar, "my reward," for her payment. Finally, Zebulun, the last of Leah's sons is born. His name means "he will respect me." Leah gives up on gaining Jacob's love; she now seeks only his respect for the six sons she has borne him. Jacob's only daughter, Dinah's, birth is recorded almost as an afterthought. There is no joy felt in the begetting of children here; only its effect on the triangle of Jacob, Leah, and Rachel is noteworthy.

At last Rachel herself gets pregnant and bears a son. Joseph, she names him, which means "may he add." Even now, Rachel is not satisfied. She does not express gratitude for finally having a child of her own, but greedily wishes for another. This wish is her undoing. In the birth of her next son, Rachel loses her own life. With her last breath, she names him Ben-oni, "the child of my misfortune." Even in the end Rachel believes that the whole affair is about her. In renaming the child Benjamin "the son of my right hand," Jacob interjects the only positive note in this whole story, finally finding joy in the child who reminds him of his love for Rachel.

It is hard to see any evidence of love in this episode in the life of the Chosen People. To call the relationship between Jacob, Rachel, and Leah a "love triangle" would be a misnomer. The major characteristics seem to be selfishness and competition. Children only seem to matter for the way they improve one or the other's position in the game. The manipulative Jacob, passive through most of this, is manipulated himself by the deception of Laban and the maneuverings of Leah and Rachel. Only in the end does Jacob take decisive action in the renaming of Benjamin, but by then it is too late; his beloved Rachel is dead, and the pattern is set for the troubled relationships of his children.

There is very little "abiding in love" in this story of Jacob and his family. His love for Rachel seems to be little more than infatuation, while the main characters of the story manipulate, trade insults, fight, and abuse each other, causing much hurt and resentment. There is no marital bliss here. No wonder that a later law (Lev 18:18) forbids a man from marrying two sisters, and later rabbinical teaching strongly recommends against polygamy for just such reasons as this torturous relationship between Jacob, Rachel, and Leah.[4]

It is easy to see the absence of God in this tale. People relying only on themselves and their own cleverness often find only heartache and deception. The subtle and not-so-subtle maneuvering of people, places, and things brings only discord. It is a sad story, a story that repeats itself over and over in countless families through the centuries. It is found when husbands and wives encounter not love and companionship, but conflict and deception. We see it when brother and sister hold on to childish resentments. It is revealed in families where children are viewed as accomplishments to be claimed rather than as joys to be cherished, or as persons in their own right. It is seen where parents live out their ambitions through the lives of their sons and daughters. Love flies from these situations, and yet love is the only remedy.

While God may seem absent to these troubled family conflicts, God also "writes straight with crooked lines." The pride that causes so many injuries within family relationships can also lead to the humility that brings reconciliation. Immature love can lead to maturity. Rivalry can give way to real communication. Love can indeed conquer all, but it takes hard work. No one ever said that love was easy. Yet, it can be found in the everyday struggles of our lives and loves. The abiding in love that signifies God's presence is not some over-spiritualized dream. It is practical. It takes day-to-day commitment to the ups and downs and realities of human relationships.

Jacob and Rachel and Leah show us how hard it is to find true love. They place in stark relief the emptiness of life without it. Unfortunately, they transmit to their children the example of rivalry, ambition, and competition that continue to make the story of Jacob's family so tragic.

Reflection Questions

1. How can families be both a help and a hindrance to experiencing the love of God in our lives?
2. What is the importance of the spoken word in the biblical story of Jacob? How does our own personal integrity affect the way we see God in others and ourselves?
3. What elements from the story of Jacob, Rachel, and Leah show the absence of love? What does this absence tell us about God?

Notes

1. Cuthbert A. Simpson, "The Book of Genesis," *The Interpreter's Bible*, Vol. I., Eds. George Arthur Buttrick, Walter Russell Bowie, et.al. Nashville: Abingdon Press, 1952, pp. 663–669, 678–684.
2. Simpson, p. 700.
3. For the meaning of the names of Jacob's sons, I have used *The New Jerome Biblical Commentary*. For variations on the meanings of these names, see: footnotes in NRSV and Jerusalem versions of the Bible.
4. Rabbi Gershom b. Judah formally forbid polygamy in c. 1000 C.E. Lavina and Dan Cohen-Sherbok, *A Popular Dictionary of Judaism*. Lincolnwood (Chicago): NTC Contemporary Publishing Company, 1995, p. 137.

CHAPTER FOUR

Joseph and His Brothers

*Now Israel loved Joseph more than
any other of his children.*

Knowing the story of Jacob and his two wives, it should not surprise us to know that their children did not get along very well. Sibling rivalry rises to new heights (or depths) in the story of Joseph and his brothers. It is a story of rivalry and hatred, of favoritism and fairness. The Scriptures describe Joseph and the other sons of Jacob in a less than flattering light, and, once again, Jacob seems unable to do anything but make the situation worse. We see unfolding in the tale of Jacob and Joseph the story of many a family over the course of history. Selfishness, arrogance, resentment, and revenge can mar family relationships. For so many, instead of being the place of comfort and strength, *family* is a word synonymous with *battlefield,* and the God communicated from one generation to the next is a God of judgment and anger—far from the God-who-is-love described in John's letter.

The narrative about Joseph paints the portraits of the main characters early in the story. The story follows the pattern set by Jacob, Rachel, and Leah. As Jacob played favorites among his wives to such destructive results, he does the same with his children. Joseph, the first-born of his beloved Rachel, receives special treatment. He comes across in the opening verses of

Genesis 37 as a spoiled and arrogant child, confident of his place of primacy in the family. Joseph's brothers, collectively, seem bloodthirsty and callow. The first reference we have about Joseph, apart from the announcement of his birth in Genesis 30:22–24, gives us more than a glimpse of his personality. At seventeen, he tattles on his older brothers. We do not know in what way his brothers were negligent in their shepherding duties, but Joseph is quick to report back to his father.

Younger children, especially in large families, do have a tendency to be tattletales. It is often a way of getting attention. Older siblings may resent the child, but usually get over it. But there was more to Joseph's relationship with his brothers than this incident shows. He was more than just an informer; he was also his father's favorite, the recipient of special gifts, including a distinctive garment—the famed "coat of many colors." Traditionally rendered as a "long robe with sleeves" (Gen 37:3), it was a princely garment that showed Jacob's favor for Joseph over and above his brothers.[1]

Now we cannot expect Jacob to be very interested in the rights of precedence for older sons. A trickster and usurper, hypocritical he is not! The older ten brothers (Benjamin, the youngest, does not appear until later) are not interested in family traditions. They feel the sting of their father's preference for Joseph. It is not a matter of who will inherit, but of who is better loved.

Certainly all parents love their children differently. The relationship of parent to child is as individual as each unique child. Usually, however, this difference is one of kind and not degree. Even children who cause heartache can claim their parents' love. We are seeing something very different here. The sense of the scriptural passage is that Jacob gave Joseph all the privileges of an only son, which filled the brothers with resentment and jealousy. Three times we are told that they hated

Joseph (Gen 37:4, 5, 8), and "could not speak peaceably with him."

Joseph does not do much to help the situation. Not only does he curry his father's favor, but acts with arrogance towards his brothers. His dreams of grandeur are couched in derogatory terms that place as much emphasis on the brothers' deficiency as on his own destiny.

Dreams are an important part of the divine milieu in the Bible. They are a favorite medium of communication between God and humanity. Dreams portray the mystery of such communication while protecting the transcendence of God. Jacob himself was a dreamer of divine messages, and in the Gospel of Matthew, Joseph, Mary's husband, responds to dreams as he guides his young family through the early years of Jesus' life.[2]

Jacob's son Joseph is a dreamer too, but also an interpreter of dreams as we find out in Genesis 40 and 41. This gift will work in Joseph's favor when he is older, but now, in relation to his family, Joseph's rendition of his two dreams in Genesis 37:5–11 serves only to cause discord and bitterness. In emphasizing the precedence of his own "star" over and above his brothers, and in interpreting the bowing sheaves as his family's subservience, Joseph alienates and distances himself from his family. Even his father reprimands him, so Joseph's arrogance must have piqued even Jacob. We can only imagine the tension that surrounded this family's dealings with one another, and why the brothers, in pasturing the flock, did so far afield from the family dwelling. Perhaps they wanted to escape the shadow of Jacob's preference for Joseph, as well as Joseph's haughty demeanor.

Just in case we think that the family discord is all Joseph's fault, however, the story moves on to show the shady side of the other sons of Jacob. When they see Joseph coming out to meet them in the pasture, they immediately begin to plot against him.

This intrigue is not the idle grumbling of a disenfranchised family. They see that Joseph is alone, no longer protected by the gaze of his father, and so they seize the opportunity to rid themselves of "this dreamer."

The ten older children of Jacob do not seem to have inherited his subtlety. Grab him, kill him, and cover it up is their modus operandi. They do not stop to consider the effect this will have on Jacob, or even if it will improve their status in his favor. They only want to be rid of the arrogant little brother.

Joseph is not without his champion, however. Reuben tries to stop the outright killing of Joseph. An editorial note in the story tells us that he wished to restore Joseph to his father in secret (perhaps only to curry favor with Jacob, or perhaps out of genuine concern for Joseph, we do not know). Later, Judah also speaks against harming Joseph, but his motivation seems more oriented toward profit than concern.

Either way, Joseph is stripped of his famous garment, the symbol of his status in his father's eyes, and thrown down a dry well. Then the true nature of his brothers' callousness is seen. Having finished with Joseph for the moment, they sit down to their meal as if nothing has happened. It is at this point that Judah comes up with the idea of selling Joseph into slavery rather than killing him, "for our brother is our own flesh" (Gen 37:27). Quite a different view of the relationship of flesh and bone than we saw in the creation stories. The Man sees the Woman as the delight of his eyes because they are of the same flesh. Here, it seems, Judah is more concerned with the legal/cultic ramifications of shedding the blood of a relative.

In any event, before the sons of Jacob have any chance of acting on their schemes, a wandering group of traders from Midian kidnap Joseph from his prison in the well, and make their own deal with a caravan going to Egypt. First Reuben, then all the brothers find Joseph missing, and they decide to carry on with a cover-up operation. Dipping their brother's robe in goat's blood, they fabricate a story about his demise at the claws of a wild animal, hoping to escape any blame in the matter.

Jacob's reaction to the news is predictable, if somewhat extreme. He mourns as if for an only child. Even now, his brothers play second to Joseph in their father's eyes. Jacob announces his intention of mourning Joseph until his own death. It is as if Jacob has nothing left in this world now that his beloved son is gone. All of his family, his possessions, and his power are meaningless to him without Joseph.

Rivalry, resentment, hatred, and revenge are the story of Joseph and his family, a story played out in many families even today. While it seems natural for there to be some discord in all families, as in all relationships, for some these problems take on a pathological character.

When parents play favorites, as Jacob did, it causes undue competition within their children. Maybe it starts when one or both parents see the potential in one child to live out a dream they have long since abandoned. Possibly these problems come from favoring one gender over the other. "Your father always wanted a son" is a cruel thing to say to a daughter. What unbalance such comments can cause in a family! Sometimes a family is blended from two, and one parent cannot come to treat the children of their spouse with the same love.

In any event, the repercussions of this favoritism on children can only be disastrous. As we see played out in the story of Joseph, hatred leads to revenge, and a cold-blooded attitude of brother toward brother, sister toward sister. While we do not see children being sold into slavery by their siblings, such hatred leads to a different kind of slavery. It is a slavery that exists whenever someone is snared in spite and resentment—a slavery of the soul. It tears apart the family and brings only unhappiness to all those involved.

It is all so subtle, too. By cutting off the brother or sister who is so resented, family members may think that they have freed themselves of the burden. Once gone, the Joseph of the family will be replaced in the affections of the parent, and life will go on. No one will miss the braggart, the black sheep, and life will be better than it was before. But the reaction of Jacob shows us that this hope is unfounded. Cutting off a family member is like amputating a limb. You may be able to go on; you may be able to function normally; but life is changed forever and the missing part is never forgotten. The emotional baggage that families carry with them—the anger, the resentment, the hatred, and the hurt—affect all their relationships within and without the family. Freedom is not found, and the burden of such broken relationships is heavy.

Where is God in all of this? It is interesting that God is not mentioned at all in Genesis 37. The loving God who created humanity with such delight is nowhere to be seen in these family squabbles. Could it be that they left no room for God? Could God bring healing to Jacob's troubled family? Does God *also* play favorites? Such questions plague humankind still. Are our human relationships, broken and troubled, signs of God's ways? On the other hand, do we project onto God our resentment and anger over our family problems, blaming God for our own inability to make peace?

The story of Jacob's family to this point leaves little room for hope. Jacob and his sons are caught in the net of sinfulness that so often afflicts our relationships. Sometimes, enmeshed in the hurt, we do not even know how to begin to reconcile with sister or brother, mother or father, friend or family member. God seems absent and deaf to our prayers, and we feel powerless and alone.

Yet, God does make an appearance in the story of Joseph. Through twenty years of rising and falling fortunes, Joseph himself comes to know and rely on God. His gift of interpreting dreams is turned to the benefit of others (see Gen 40–41). Joseph rises to power in Egypt and is responsible for the country's abundance in a time of famine. When his ten brothers, the very ones who stripped him of his coat and threw him down a well, come begging for food to bring back to the land of Canaan for Jacob and his family, Joseph is in the position to take his revenge, and at first it seems that is what he will do. He keeps his true identity a secret, and speaks to his brothers only through an interpreter (Gen 42:23).

Joseph treats his brothers harshly. He accuses them of spying on Egypt. He gives them grain, but arranges to keep Simeon as a hostage against their return to Canaan. He insists that Benjamin (his younger brother, also a child of Rachel's) be brought to him in Egypt as well. It looks like business as usual between Joseph and his brothers. Trickery and deception are again at work.

All these intrigues come to a surprising end when Joseph finally reveals his identity to his brothers amid tears of forgiveness and repentance. The family is reunited as Jacob comes to Egypt and settles in the land of Goshen (Gen 46:6–7). The family of Jacob finds peace at last, as they put behind them the deeds of the past.

It is remarkable that this family could find reconciliation after all they had done to each other. But the adversity that came to Joseph, the grief that came to Jacob, and the maturity that eventually came to the brothers as a result of their actions has changed them. In the end, the brothers are willing to sacrifice themselves for the sake of Benjamin, so as to bring no new grief to Jacob. Joseph finds it in his heart to forgive them, and even sees how good has come from their bad actions. Jacob finally finds himself at the center of a united family.

Is this kind of reconciliation possible for families torn by resentment and hatred? Is there a way out of the slavery that such painful family relations cause? The key, it seems, is forgiveness. Where there is the willingness to forgive, God can bring healing. The forgiveness that can bring such resolution to families like Jacob's is a hard-won reality. It is not accomplished by a simple apology, nor by letting bygones be bygones. A lot of work has to be done to assuage the hurt and repair the damage.

Both Joseph and his brothers had to change before they could come together in forgiveness. Both parties had to let go of the past hurts that they could no longer change, and reach out to each other. Reconciliation is a two-way street. It is not an overnight process. Years of living life's vicissitudes must go by before people realize how useless it is to hold on to past hurts. Sometimes tragedy has to occur before people understand how important and freeing forgiveness is. Some hurts are harder to let go of than others. Nor is forgiveness an invitation to further abuse. Yet, the human heart's power to open up even to those who have broken it is itself a sign of God's presence. Moreover, where the God of love is present, all things are possible.

Reflection Questions

1. How does Jacob play favorites among his children? What effect does favoritism have on family relationships? Do you think that God plays favorites? Why or why not?

2. How can one bring reconciliation into family situations of hurt and resentment?

7

3. What work and change needs to happen within in order to forgive deep hurts? What needs to happen to be forgiven?

Notes

1. Gerhard Von Rad. *Genesis*. Trans. John H. Manks. Philadelphia: The Westminster Press, 1961, p. 364.
2. Von Rad, pp. 346–347. Bruce Vawter. *On Genesis: A New Reading*. Garden City: Doubleday & Company, Inc., 1977, p. 383.

CHAPTER FIVE

Ruth and Boaz

So Boaz took Ruth and she became his wife.

In the midst of the brokenness of human relationships, of abuse, tragedy, and inequality, some stories of genuine love do survive—love that blossoms despite adversity and rises above the obstacles that life puts in its way. Such is the story of Ruth and Boaz, the story of two people of substance who find each other and find love.

The Book of Ruth is a book about human relationships. The locus of God's activity is in and through human activity, as if to say God's presence can be seen only behind and beneath the actions and relationships of the human characters. There are five main protagonists in this work: Naomi, the widow, around whom the issues of this story gather; Ruth and Orpah, her daughters-in-law; Boaz, a man of substance, and an unnamed kinsman, both of whose responses to Naomi and Ruth frame the message of the book.

The story of Ruth is a story about covenant. Covenant is an important theme in the Hebrew Scriptures. It expresses the relationship of God to humanity, and of human to human. Covenant holds the measuring stick to all of our human activities. Does this or that action measure up to the goal of the covenant? This goal, in Hebrew, is called *hesed. Hesed* is loosely translated as love or charity or, more precisely, as loving faithfulness.[1] It is the love that goes beyond the expected and brings goodness, rightness, hope, and fulfillment. *Hesed* is behind the promise "I will be your God, and you shall be my people" (cf. Lev 26:12; Jer 7:23; 30:22; Ezek 36:28). It is seen in times of punishment, such as the famine that drives Elimelech and his family into Moab (Ruth 1:1), and in times of plenty, such as Boaz experiences (Ruth 2:1ff). Primarily, however, it is seen in the interactions of Ruth and Orpah with Naomi, and in the response of Boaz and the unnamed kinsman to Ruth. In every scene of this delightful story the question is asked, "Who is making the *hesed*-based decision?"

The story is placed "In the days when the judges ruled..." (Ruth 1:1), though scholars believe that Ruth was written in the post-exilic period as a protest to the strict stance against intermarriage taken by Ezra and Nehemiah.[2] The main character, Ruth, is a citizen of Moab, a neighbor of Israel and not a member of the covenant community. She is a foreigner. By making her an ancestor of King David, the locus of messianic hopes, the author of Ruth is making a statement against the prohibition forbidding marriage between Jews and non-Jews found in Ezra 9:1–4; 10:6–44, and again in Nehemiah 13:23–30. The sacred author is saying that the covenant with God is open-ended, and that covenant-*hesed* can be seen even in the lives and actions of foreigners.

The narrative begins with the flight of the family of Elimelech from famine-stricken Israel. He takes his wife, Naomi, and two sons into neighboring Moab. There Elimelech dies. His sons, Mahlon and Chilion marry Moabite women, Orpah and Ruth, respectively, and they settle down to live their lives. Mahlon and Chilion die childless, however, and all three women are now widows. In the patriarchal society of eleventh century B.C., widows were quite powerless—the object of charity.[3]

Naomi, a foreigner in Moab, can expect little help, and so determines to go back to Israel where the famine has ended.

Orpah and Ruth are still young women, and they can expect the possibility of finding new husbands among their own people. Both Ruth and Orpah offer to accompany Naomi back to Israel because of their love for their mother-in-law. Naomi refuses to let them, telling them to stay with their countrymen. Orpah, amid tears of farewell and genuine affection, kisses Naomi goodbye and departs. Ruth, however, does the unexpected. In an act of self-renunciation that can only be understood in the context of covenant-*hesed*, Ruth joins her destiny to that of Naomi. She turns her back on country, family, and even her gods, and places herself at the mercy of the God of Israel. She says, "Your people will be my people and your God my God" (Ruth 1:16). Thus Ruth becomes more than daughter-in-law, she takes the role of true daughter. Nor is she doing this action in expectation of any reward, for Naomi has nothing to give. What Ruth does can only be motivated by love.

Ruth's character is established here in relation to Orpah through their responses to Naomi. Orpah has done nothing wrong in returning to her people. Her fondness for Naomi is not in question. Her offer to accompany her mother-in-law back to Israel is itself a loving offer. But in returning to her people, Orpah does what is expected. Ruth, on the other hand, goes beyond what is expected. She commits herself to taking care of Naomi, the widow. She takes the task that is God's as protector of the powerless, the widow, and orphan (see Ps 141:9). Ruth, the foreigner, by nature understands the *hesed* expected of the covenant people and their God.

So when Ruth and Boaz meet in chapter two, her good reputation precedes her. Boaz is described as a wealthy man—a man of substance both materially and morally. Even the relationship he has with his workers shows him to be a man of fairness and respect (Ruth 2:4). The good Boaz recognizes the goodness in Ruth, and he rewards her appropriately. He, too, goes beyond what might be expected of a generous man and not only allows Ruth to glean in his fields for grain, but makes the job easier for her. He even permits her to drink from the workers' water supply (Ruth 2:9). Already Boaz sees that Ruth is a woman worthy of attention, but the drama of this story is only beginning.

In order to understand the next section of the Book of Ruth, we need to explore the ancient Levirite law of Israel. In a tribal society such as Israel, keeping property in the family is important, but only males could own property. If a man died childless, or without a male heir, then what would happen to his property? Very likely it could pass out of the family and thus reduce the tribal wealth. If a man died, therefore, without a son, it was in the best interest of the family to find a way to provide him with one. The Levirite law was aimed at this situation.

The brother, or near kinsman of a man who died without an heir, was expected to marry their kinsman's widow and raise children up in his name. The first son of this union would technically be seen in the eyes of the law as the legal heir of the dead man, and his property would be kept in the family. Thus his name would not die out from the annals of tribal history. The source of this law is found in Deuteronomy 25:5–10, but the word *brother* here is taken in its broadest context. Any close kinsman would be termed *brother* in ancient Levirite law. The story of covenant-*hesed* now unfolds in Ruth in the context of this Levirite law.[4]

When Naomi finds out that Boaz has favored Ruth in her gleaning of grain, she realizes that he is a kinsman of her dead husband and his sons, and that the Levirite custom might be invoked. She comes up with a plan for Ruth, so that Boaz may assume his role as "redeemer." Because of his reputation for justice, Naomi is confident that Boaz will do the right thing so she sends Ruth to him.

Ruth comes to the threshing floor of Boaz after dark. Having finished his day's work, and content in his successful harvest, Boaz eats and drinks and lies down to sleep without a worry. Ruth comes to him and "uncovers his feet" (Ruth 3:7). The term *feet* is often used euphemistically in the Hebrew Scriptures to mean *genitals*. This scene is filled with sexual innuendo and mystery. Just what happened at the threshing floor of Boaz? Is Ruth trying to place Boaz in a compromising position, and by doing so force his hand? We have to see this episode in the context of who Ruth and Boaz are, and the values that have characterized their actions up to this point. Both Ruth and Boaz are people of substance. Ruth has been self-sacrificing and more than scrupulous in living out the ideal of *hesed*. Boaz has been generous and has been presented as a man of uprightness and justice. Would either of these people choose a less than proper way of pursuing their relationship? As the episode at the threshing floor comes to its conclusion, these questions are not only *not* answered equivocally, but the actions of Boaz toward Ruth continue to show his respect for her, as well as his just-mindedness.

Upon discovering Ruth lying beside him, Boaz asks, "Who are you?" (Ruth 3:8). Previously, when he first saw her in the field, Boaz had asked to whom Ruth belonged (2:5), betraying the mindset of the patriarchal time that saw women as possessions. Now, confronted by the woman herself, Boaz has no choice but to see Ruth as a person with whom he must deal personally. It is only in this context that Ruth makes her request. Not because of duty as her dead husband's relative, but because of who she is and what she has accomplished does Ruth claim of Boaz the right of marriage under the Levirite law.[5]

"Spread your cloak over your servant..." (Ruth 3:9) is a statement that harks back to Boaz's wish for Ruth in 2:12. If Boaz truly wishes the Lord to take Ruth under the protection "of his wings," Boaz himself will have to supply those wings. Once again, we see that God's presence is seen only through the actions and interactions of the human participants of the story.

Boaz responds to Ruth's request and applauds her actions. She has shown herself both resourceful and righteous. She has chosen a more difficult path towards security—a riskier path— and Boaz can only respond with respect and righteousness himself. Righteousness, however, requires that Boaz acknowledge the claim of a nearer kinsman. Ruth's dead husband has a relative of closer ties who, under the Levirite law, has a prior claim on Ruth and the property of Elimelech. That he has not already come forth may indicate what sort of person he is, but that remains to be seen as the drama of this story plays itself out.

Once decided on a course of action, Boaz does not hesitate to conclude it. Further, he makes sure that the matter is done with all righteousness according to the law and custom of his people. So that his actions are legal in the eyes of the community, he gathers ten elders to act as witnesses to the transaction. Boaz asks this unnamed kinsman if he wishes to "redeem" or buy the land belonging to Elimelech—the sale of which would provide sustenance for Naomi, while adding to the family inheritance of the kinsman. This next-of-kin is willing to do so, but when he finds out that marriage to Ruth is involved, meaning that the land would become the inheritance of her son alone, he is unwilling to do so. Thus his claim to both land and marriage is given up, and this action frees Boaz to marry Ruth.

Once again, we see a contrast between the actions of Boaz and the actions of the kinsman. The man does nothing wrong. For whatever reason, marriage with Ruth would be difficult for him, and so he gives up his claim and all within the righteousness of the law. Yet we see in Boaz's actions that he is willing to go farther than the precepts of the law, and makes a choice based on *hesed*. Boaz's generosity, fairness, and courage are underscored by the actions of the unnamed nearer kinsman in the same way that Ruth is seen in light of Orpah's actions earlier in the story. Ruth and Boaz, then, are seen as people of similar values who go the extra step to make the *hesed*-based decisions. It is out of this union of two "people of substance" that the line of King David comes. This union is a sign of God's *hesed*-love for Israel.

The story of Ruth and Boaz is more than just an ancient tale of the history of Israel. It is a story that reminds us that true love—the love in which God abides—is love that goes the extra distance. It is love that sacrifices and takes risks and that allows itself to be vulnerable. It is love that trusts. Ruth trusts that her love for Naomi will bear fruit, and that her love for Boaz will triumph. Boaz trusts that in doing the right thing in the right way he will not lose the woman of substance that he has discovered.

We learn a lot from this story. We see it played out in the lives of families even today. We see it in men and women who stick to their values when searching for a partner in life, who are willing to go beyond the expectations of society about love and marriage and wait for lasting love. These are people who are willing to put the hard work into their relationships that ensures such longevity. We see this love in the sacrifices of parents for their children, in the way brothers and sisters help each other throughout life, and in the fidelity of spouses to each other in the changing patterns of their lives.

The love of Boaz and Ruth acknowledges the sexual tensions and attractions that are present in their relationship, but challenges us to see beyond the physical and sexual side of their love to the solid love built upon shared values and faith.

Wherever people seek out a soulmate who is both friend and lover, we witness the love of Ruth and Boaz lived again, and in this love story we see God present. God is present in the individuals that make the choices and in the love that draws the persons together. Ruth finds the God of Israel in her love for Naomi, and that faith is confirmed in the actions of Boaz towards her. Boaz finds that his commitment to justice and righteousness leads to fulfillment in his relationship with Ruth.

God is, indeed, present in the decisions we make. God's love, covenant-*hesed*, is seen over and over when we go beyond the expected to be loving, strong, and faithful to our values in the face of opposition and hardship. God is found in loving relationships, and God sustains loving relationships. Loving relationships are the expression of God's presence and the sign of hope that God is love.

Reflection Questions

1. What does it mean to have a "covenant relationship" with God? How does this covenant express itself in human relationships?
2. What "*hesed*-based" decisions does Ruth make? Boaz? How do these decisions bring them together?
3. What values are important to your life? How do these values dictate your actions?

Notes

1. Alice A. Laffey, "Ruth," *The New Jerome Biblical Commentary*. Eds. Raymond E. Brown, S.S., Joseph A. Fitzmyer, S.J. and Roland E. Murphy, O. Carm. Englewood Cliffs, NJ: Prentice Hall, Inc., 1990, p. 554.
2. John Craghan. *Esther, Judith, Tobit, Jonah, Ruth*. Old Testament Message, vol. 16. Eds. Carroll Stuhlmueller and

Martin McNamara. Wilmington: Michael Glazier, Inc., 1982, p. 201.
3. John L. McKenzie, S.J. *Dictionary of the Bible.* New York: MacMillan Publishing Company, 1965, p. 927.
4. McKenzie, p. 506.
5. Laffey, pp. 556–57.

CHAPTER SIX

David and Jonathan

Jonathan loved David as his own soul.

So far, in our perusal of scriptural love stories, we have limited ourselves to family situations. Now we turn to that type of love we call friendship. All of us have people in our lives that we consider "close friends." We are privileged, however, when we have someone we can call our *"best* friend." Our "best friend" is a person with whom we can be ourselves, someone who brings out the best in us. Such a companion is a rare and wonderful find. While sometimes the person we call "best friend" is a family member or spouse, most often it is someone who is outside our family circle, someone whose loyalty and support builds us up and inspires us. It is usually an individual whom we choose to have as part of our lives. Friendship is a special kind of love.

There are many examples of friendship in the Bible, yet none is more touching than that of David and Jonathan recounted in the First Book of Samuel. David was the great-grandson of Ruth and Boaz. He was a shepherd boy who very early in life rose to fame and greatness. Jonathan was the eldest son of King Saul, the first king of Israel. He was the heir apparent to the throne of all Israel. David is known in Scripture as a poet, musician, prophet, military leader, and king. Jonathan is mentioned more briefly and is eclipsed by the brighter star of his friend. Yet he had a profound impact on David's life. While we often see David as a very complex man, at once ambitious and humble, spiritual and sinful, great and weak, his friendship with Jonathan brings out the best in him.

Jonathan's story can only be told in the context of the founding of the monarchy in Israel, and of David's rise to power. Saul, Jonathan's father, is truly one of the most tragic figures in history. Acclaimed king by the people, he seemed reluctant to take on the burdens of kingship (see 1 Sam 9:1–10:24), and yet, once David begins to be popular, Saul is equally reluctant to let go of any of his royal prerogatives.

In its early stages, the Hebrew monarchy was not necessarily a hereditary right. Saul was an "elected" king, chosen by both God and the people. It was by no means certain that his son Jonathan would succeed him. Saul may have dreamed of founding a dynasty, but could do so only through the consent of the people and the blessing of God. A century or so later, long after Saul's reign, when the ten northern tribes rebelled against Solomon's son Rehoboam, they quote this principle as they set up the Northern Kingdom of Israel. Thus, when young David began to rise in popularity with the people, Saul sees him as a threat to his kingship, and the potential kingship of his son. His jealousy and paranoia frame all of Saul's attempts to rid himself of the young David.

David came to prominence as a very young person. Two traditions are intertwined in 1 Samuel to tell us how David came into Saul's service. One emphasizes David as an artist. His music and singing soothe the rages and headaches that plagued Saul in his latter years (1 Sam 16:19–23). Another strand emphasizes David as a prodigy of strength and military skill. Even as a boy, he defeats the Philistine giant, Goliath, and as a young man, he becomes one of Saul's most important and successful war-leaders (1 Sam 17:32–51).

Either way, very early in the story we see Saul's jealousy of David as a potential source of deadly conflict. It would not have been surprising had Jonathan shared his father's distrust of David. David's successes and personal popularity were a threat to any aspiration that Jonathan may have entertained regarding the throne. Yet, the friendship that develops between David and Jonathan rises above the concerns of country, government, or even personal ambition.

Jonathan meets David just after David's victory over the Philistine champion, Goliath. From the very first, Jonathan and David find a spark of friendship that defines their relationship.

> The soul of Jonathan was bound to the soul of David, and Jonathan loved him as his own soul. (1 Sam 18:1)

The love they share for one another binds their souls together. It seems that in each other David and Jonathan have found kindred spirits, and immediately make a covenant of friendship (1 Sam 18:3). Jonathan clothes David in his robe and armor. This action describes some type of covenant ritual, but, in effect, it amounts to an abdication on Jonathan's part to any claim over the kingship. In the light of subsequent actions between the two, Jonathan has recognized the ascendancy of David, and his love for his new friend expresses itself in the sacrifice of his own ambition to be king.[1]

The relationship of Jonathan and David is put into relief by Saul's increasing animosity toward the young hero. In fact, 1 Samuel 18 shows how Saul, Jonathan, and Saul's daughter, Michal, individually make a choice regarding David. Saul chooses jealousy and fear, while Jonathan and Michal choose love and friendship. In this context, we see the larger picture of Saul's rejection as king of Israel and David's rise to favor in the eyes of Jonathan, Michal, and the people. This favor confirms the election of David by God as destined king of the chosen people (1 Sam 16:1–13). The friendship of David and Jonathan continues throughout the first book of Samuel. Jonathan takes David's part with his father in 1 Samuel 19:1–6, and in 1 Samuel 20, we again witness the self-sacrifice and loyalty of Jonathan for his friend.

Loyalty, of course, is the most apparent of Jonathan's characteristics. Having made a covenant with David, Jonathan realizes that fidelity to his friend is the bond and the seal of that relationship. Jonathan's choices throughout the rest of his life are made in faithfulness to this covenant. His love for David is expressed in the way he deals with his own father and in the way he warns David of the impending plans for his destruction at the hands of Saul.

Jonathan says to his friend David, "May the Lord be with you as he was with my father" (1 Sam 20:13), and he works and plans for David's escape from Saul. Jonathan once again abdicates his claim to royal prerogative in favor of David. The Lord chooses Israel's king, and if he is with David as he was with Saul, then Jonathan has no hope of becoming king. Jonathan recognizes that the patronage of God has left Saul, and he wishes these blessings to descend upon David rather than himself. How different this relationship is from that of Jacob and Esau. Jacob robs his brother of Isaac's blessing by deceit while Jonathan freely gives his to David because he recognizes God's hand is upon his young friend. His love for David wishes only the best of blessings for him. The only thing asked in return is David's loyalty to Jonathan's family when David is king—a vow David fulfills when he takes care of Jonathan's crippled son, Meriboseth (2 Sam 9:1–13).

Thus far, however, David has been passive in his friendship with Jonathan. Jonathan is the loyal and loving friend who sacrifices self and future for the sake of David, while David has been only the recipient of Jonathan's actions. What kind of friendship does David provide?

We do not see David's side of the friendship until after Jonathan's death. A case could be made that up to this point, David's actions toward Jonathan have been manipulative,[2] using him to advance David's own ambitions, ambitions that are thwarted when David flees into the wilderness and becomes an outlaw in Israel. Saul's hatred, jealousy, and persecution, so in contrast with Jonathan's attitude, have cut David off from communication with his friend. David pursues his career as a bandit in the hills of Judah, all the while gathering around him a band of loyal followers. Jonathan continues as heir apparent, and also leader of Saul's army. Only after word of the defeat of Saul and Jonathan, and their death on Mt. Gilboa (1 Sam 31), comes to David do we witness the depth of his attachment to both Jonathan and Saul. The "Elegy of David" over Saul and Jonathan is an emotionally moving example of David's art as a poet. In this brief lament, David pours out all of his soul, and bares his feelings for the two men who have touched his life in such a profound way.

This poem, commonly thought to have come directly from David himself, with very little editing by later redactors, over-flows with honest grief, while at the same time recognizing how limited words are to express such sorrow.[3] David realizes that the death of Saul and Jonathan is an occasion for distress not only for himself, but also for all of Israel. David looks past Saul's violent behavior towards him and emphasizes the great deeds Saul has performed in the service of Israel, not the least of which was drawing together the various tribes in national and religious unity—a work that David would continue. He says:

> Saul and Jonathan, beloved and lovely!
> In life and death they were not divided;

they were swifter than eagles,
    they were stronger than lions.

Daughters of Israel, weep over Saul,
    who clothed you with crimson, in luxury,
    who put ornaments of gold on your apparel.

How the mighty have fallen
    in the midst of battle! (2 Sam 1:23–25)

David saves the last part of his lament for his friend Jonathan.[4] He describes Jonathan as a kindred spirit, for whom he had a special devotion. The friendship that they shared, David says, was more meaningful to him than any of the relationships with his many wives. David recognizes that his friendship with Jonathan was the defining relationship of his life. He mourns:

I am distressed for you, my brother Jonathan;
greatly beloved were you to me;
    your love to me was wonderful,
    passing the love of women. (2 Sam 1:26)

This elegy shows a genuineness not always seen in David because of his ambition and pride. In this lament, however, he expresses his true friendship for Jonathan, which transcended ambition, greed, and personal gain. Jonathan has, even in death, brought out the best in David.

Bringing out the best in another is a determining quality of friendship. When I am with a good friend, I am able to let down my guard. Friendships allow us to be ourselves, but more; friends call us to growth and challenge us to reach for new heights. A friend is both a mirror and a sounding board, someone who reflects our true selves back to us, and helps us to figure out which path to take in the jumbling confusion of life's choices.

A friend is loyal. No matter what I do or where I go, my friends stand by me. Yet, this loyalty is not passive acceptance of my behaviors when these are destructive. A friend will challenge, set boundaries, and not be afraid to be tough at times, all at the service of helping. A friend's loyalty will take the risk of anger, or even the possibility of losing the friendship, for the benefit of the loved one. This kind of faithfulness inspires a similar commitment, which is the bond that allows friendship to grow.

Friendship stands the test of time and distance. Very early in their relationship, David and Jonathan are separated by the animosity of Saul; yet, their friendship remains an important part of their lives, and even after Jonathan's death, it moves David and affects his actions. Theirs was a friendship that lasted. Some relationships come and go, but a best friend, a soulmate, will be part of our lives even though far away. These types of relationships can go years without contact, and still pick up immediately when again they meet. Even through the changes that life brings their way, friends grow closer together, and even if separated by death, the memory of a best friend still motivates us with love and inspires us with devotion.

The love that is friendship is a sure sign of God's presence and action. The bond that draws people together, helps them to find common ground, and allows them to open their hearts to one another is a special grace. It is a sacrament of the friendship we can attain with God. Loyalty, and the ability to bring out the best that's in us, are qualities of our relationship with God that often reveal themselves in our human friendships. Like the friendship between Jonathan and David, true friendship is a covenant of love that moves us closer to understanding the God-who-is-love.

Reflection Questions

1. How have friendships impacted your life?
2. How would you characterize the differences in attitude toward David from Saul and Jonathan?
3. How does Jonathan's friendship bring out the best in David? What does that say about true friendship?

Notes

1. Walter Brueggemann. *First and Second Samuel.* Interpretation. Ed., James Luther Mays. Louisville: John Knox Press, 1990, p. 136; Robert P. Gordon. *I and II Samuel.* Grand Rapids: Zondervan Publishing House, 1986, p. 159.
2. K. L. Knoll, "The Faces of David," *Journal of Study of Old Testament,* Supplement Series 242. Eds., David J. A. Clissis and Phillip R. Davies. Sheffield, England: Sheffield Academic Press, 1997, p. 81.
3. Brueggemann, *First and Second Samuel,* p. 213.
4. Gordon, p. 212.

CHAPTER SEVEN

Hosea and Gomer

Therefore I will allure her...
and speak tenderly to her.

We saw in the friendship of David and Jonathan that covenanted love is based on loyalty and fidelity. What happens, however, when that faithfulness is broken? Does the covenant end when one party is unfaithful to it? These questions have practical implications in the lives and loves of people. Betrayal of friendship and unfaithfulness in marriage are sources of much heartbreak. Men and women who promise love, loyalty, and mutual support, and then break their promises, not only hurt their partners, but damage the fundamental trust that allows people to reach out and take the risk of loving. Abiding in love becomes a harsh joke to people who have been hurt by the lovers they thought were true.

Can healing be found in the lives of those who have been so hurt? Can love survive and rise above the disappointment, anger, and betrayal? Where is God to be found in the lives of the brokenhearted? Such questions are addressed, if not entirely answered, in the life and prophecies of Hosea, who lived and worked in the seventh century B.C. in the Northern Kingdom of Israel.[1]

Hosea's message was a challenge and a call to faithfulness on the part of the Chosen People to their God. Israel itself had broken the covenant with God, syncretized their religious practices with that of the Canaanites, and had begun to depend solely on their own religious practices combined with that of the Canaanites, and to depend solely on their own wealth and security. Hosea's prophecies cut through these exterior successes of Israel and its monarchy to reveal the depth of the Israelite society's need to return to God and the ways of God's law. Hosea called people back to their covenant faithfulness because not only their worship of false gods had broken it, but also because their attachment to material prosperity was idolatrous. Hosea perceived clearly that Israel's infidelity to their covenant relationship with God would lead swiftly to their ruin. The great empire of Assyria was perched on the borders of Israel, and the policies and practices of both king and people wcre speeding the day when Assyria would destroy them.

The message of Hosea, however, cannot be separated from the story of his life and marriage. His insight into the damage that Israel's unfaithfulness was doing to the people came from his own experiences of a faithless wife. He realized that his love for his wife, even when she had betrayed him, was an image of God's love for the wayward people of Israel—a love that called them back to commitment and wanted only their healing. Hosea's own heartbreak gave him an intuition about the love of God.

Because the story of Hosea's marriage is intimately entwined with his prophecy to the people, it is difficult to separate Hosea's life-experience from his prophetic message, and tell the story simply.[2] It seems that God commands Hosea to enter into a faithless marriage:

> ...the Lord said to Hosea, "Go, take for yourself a wife of whoredom and have children of whoredom, for the land commits great whoredom by forsaking the Lord." (Hos 1:2)

The context of the story as it unfolds, however, leads us to believe that Hosea's wife, Gomer, became unfaithful only *after* their marriage and the birth of their children. It is only in hindsight that Hosea sees his relationship with Gomer as symbolic of God's relationship with the people of Israel.

Further, it is unclear what kind of unfaithfulness "whoredom" means. The Hebrew word used by Hosea is not the usual one for a prostitute.[3] It has the connotation of the type of harlotry connected with the ritual worship of the Canaanite god, Baal. Was Gomer participating in the temple prostitution of the Canaanite fertility rites? If this is the situation, then her unfaithfulness to Hosea is twofold. Not only is she sexually unfaithful, but by also committing idolatry she has broken her covenant with him as a faithful follower of the Lord. She has betrayed his trust and his faith. On the other hand, did Gomer merely commit adultery, maybe several times, and it is Hosea who makes the connection with the idolatry of the people?

These questions are still the subject of scholarly debate, but not, however, Hosea's reaction to Gomer's infidelity. He is hurt, disappointed, and angry. Her actions have devastated him. Gomer has betrayed his love, and Hosea is at a loss as to how to deal with it. Maybe only someone who has known this kind of breach of faith can understand the depth of Hosea's emotions: his anger, pain, and resentment. How can he faithfully respond to Gomer's unfaithfulness? At first he says to his children:

> Plead with your mother, plead—
> > for she is not my wife,
> > and I am not her husband—
> that she put away her whoring from her face,
> > and her adultery from between her breasts.
> > (Hos 2:2)

Throughout these passages, as Hosea attempts to deal with his relationship with Gomer, there is a remarkable quality. Although she has hurt him severely, Hosea seems willing to have reconciliation. His first reaction is to plead, to beg Gomer to stop her unfaithfulness. He recognizes that her behavior has destroyed their marriage, but is willing to take her back. His love for her is a faithful love, even when Gomer's has not been.

Yet, there is still anger. If she does not return to him and put aside her infidelity, Hosea threatens her with retribution.

...I will strip her naked
    and expose her as in the day she was born,
and make her like a wilderness,
    and turn her into a parched land,
    and kill her with thirst. (Hos 2:3)

But even his anger gives way to another plan. Rather than punish her out of vengeance, Hosea wishes to bring her to her senses. Gomer believes that her other lovers, whoever they may be, will take care of her. Perhaps she even thinks it is they who have provided for her needs from the beginning. This last point would be especially true if her adultery were connected with the Canaanite fertility cult. If Gomer were in some way connected with the institution of temple prostitution and the Baal worship that was part of Canaanite religious ritual, she could possibly hope for a livelihood from that quarter. Hosea realizes, however, that these people do not really love Gomer; indeed, that they have been using her. So he proposes to make her realize that his love for her is her true hope and way of life.

He proposes to punish her, but not for retribution. Hosea wants Gomer to see the error of her ways, and come back to him. He says:

Therefore I will hedge up her way with thorns;
    and I will build a wall against her,
    so that she cannot find her paths.
She shall pursue her lovers,
    but not overtake them;
and she shall seek them,
    but shall not find them.
Then she shall say, "I will go
    and return to my first husband,
    for it was better with me then than now."
She did not know
    that it was I who gave her
    the grain, the wine, and the oil,
and who lavished upon her silver
    and gold that they used for Baal. (Hos 2:6–8)

Hosea seems to be taking the stand of "tough love." He will remove support from his faithless wife and make things difficult for her, but not to exact vengeance. Hosea only wishes to make Gomer realize that her other "lovers" do not really love her. They have been using her for their pleasure. If she comes to them in need, they will not support her. Left with nowhere else to go, Hosea hopes that Gomer will begin to reminisce about her times with him. Things were better because Hosea treated her with kindness and love. Could it be his love would win her back? Hosea gave her everything she had that was good and valuable in the first place. When she realizes it, just maybe Gomer will fall in love with Hosea again. Hosea hopes that by making things difficult for Gomer, she will realize the falseness of her other "lovers." Faithless love is no love at all.

Hosea's plan, however, is not all negative. He intends to be proactive as well in winning Gomer back. He says:

Therefore, I will now allure her,
    and bring her into the wilderness,
    and speak tenderly to her.
From there I will give her her vineyards,
    and make the Valley of Achor a door of hope.
There she shall respond as in the days of her youth,
    as at the time when she came out of the land of
      Egypt.
    On that day, says the LORD, you will call me, "My
husband," and no longer will you call me, "My Baal."
    For I will remove the names of the Baals from her
mouth, and they shall be mentioned by name no more.
    I will make for you a covenant on that day with the
wild animals, the birds of the air, and the creeping
things of the ground; and I will abolish the bow, the
sword, and war from the land; and I will make you lie
down in safety.
    And I will take you for my wife forever; I will take
you for my wife in righteousness and in justice, in
steadfast love, and in mercy.
    I will take you for my wife in faithfulness; and you
shall know the LORD. (Hos 2:14–20)

Obviously this passage combines Hosea's experience with
his expression of God's hope for the people of Israel. Yet it also
shows the depth of Hosea's feelings. Not only will he try to
make Gomer see how faithless her other lovers are, but he
wants to show her how faithful he can be. He will woo her
again, and hopefully she will respond as in the days of her
youth, when Gomer and Hosea were in their early love. Hosea
has not forgotten the love that brought them together. Maybe if
Gomer experiences it again, she will turn to him and call him
her husband once more.

We do not know how the story of Hosea and Gomer worked
out. The Book of Hosea is much more concerned with the rela-

tionship of Israel and God than with the relationship of Hosea the prophet and his wife Gomer. Perhaps Gomer and Hosea achieved reconciliation, perhaps not. In chapter three of Hosea, the text hints that Hosea married Gomer again—paying the bride price for her (Hosea 3:1–2). Regardless, his love for her and willingness to take her back and forgive her is evident in his writings. It is this sensitivity in Hosea that made him such a poignant spokesman for the Lord. His broken heart allowed him to perceive the great love of God for the people. Hosea understood that abiding in love could be painful and filled with uncertainty.

In an age when so many marriages fail, it is not difficult to relate to the painful emotions that Hosea experienced in his relationship with Gomer. The hopefulness of new lovers, the joy and the excitement of the newly married, all turn cold in the face of unfaithfulness and broken promises. Hosea's anger and hurt, his initial desire to exact vengeance, are natural responses for anyone who has been betrayed. It would be understandable if Hosea had turned his back on Gomer, dismissed her from his life, and moved on to other things. Such actions, however, are never quite so easy. Hosea had children to think about and care for, and somewhere, deep inside, his love for Gomer had not died. He could not turn his back on her, even though she had done so to him. Hosea wanted to find a way to turn her around again, and bring her back. He was not willing to accept her infidelities, but was willing to forgive and start over with her. Hosea was not a victim who would allow Gomer to hurt him again and again, but he did realize that his love for her—covenant love—could not so easily be dismissed. While he would "hedge her way with thorns" (Hos 2:6) to prevent further unfaithfulness, he also wanted to guide her back to him, believing that his love would bring healing to their relationship.

Several factors are at play in Hosea's actions. One has to do with his view of the covenant relationship itself. Hosea understands marriage to be a covenant, an image of the covenant between God and Israel. As human beings are created in God's image and likeness, our human relationships also portray that reality. Hosea is a man of deep religious convictions, and he recognizes that God is always faithful to the people created in the divine image. No matter what, God is constant. The goal and ideal of covenant is faithfulness, regardless of the circumstance. Hosea believed that even though Gomer had been unfaithful, he had to remain faithful to his covenant promises.

For Hosea, then, covenant is much more than a contract. Once broken, a contract is null and void, but a covenant is a more profound reality. While a contract can be termed a fifty-fifty agreement, covenant requires one-hundred percent commitment. Hosea was not willing to give up so easily on this relationship. Based on love, not on law, Hosea does not seek a way out of his commitment, but hopes that love will bring healing.

Is Hosea's idealism unrealistic? In the post-sexual revolution world, where sex is casual and unfaithfulness often presumed to be the norm, such faithfulness on the part of Hosea might seem naive. The lived reality of betrayed trust, hurt feelings, and devastated hope often precludes any discussion of reconciliation. Can a trust once broken ever be given again? Hosea's struggles with these issues are not answered in his writings. His prophecies merely raise the possibilities.

Moreover, what can we say of God in the midst of this brokenness? Hosea's spiritual insight is sublime. God is portrayed as a lover and humanity as God's beloved. If people's sin and infidelity have betrayed God's love, then God is indeed close to the brokenhearted (Ps 34:18). In a world as yet unfinished, filled with broken promises and broken dreams, God knows and shares our feelings. God knows how difficult our lives and relationships can be. If the ideal is forgiveness and reconciliation, maybe it is an ideal we cannot, by ourselves, achieve. Maybe it is only something for which we strive. There are limits to our human capacity to love, but not God's. The message of Hosea is clear: God waits for our return and God's love is constant. Forgiveness is possible. Covenant love has no strings attached.

In many ways this subject is the most difficult to write about. The strong emotions that accompany shattered relationships often prevent us from being able to forgive. Sometimes they block our ability to move on. There is a great reality to the metaphor "broken heart." The part of our spirit that we call our heart can truly be damaged by past relationships. Those people who have hurt us can own a little piece of us. We can easily dwell in the pain and memory of woundedness. The commitment of covenant love leaves us vulnerable to this kind of wound. Love requires risk-taking, and risk-taking can be dangerous. To take the chance to abide in love is also to take the chance of feeling unloved. God can seem absent, and true love an illusion, when our spirits are hurt by unfaithfulness and damaged relationships.

Yet our faith calls us to believe in possibilities beyond our reach. If God indeed is love, then love can work miracles and bring healing and hope where brokenness and despair seem unconquerable.

Reflection Questions

1. What can we learn from Hosea's actions and attitudes toward Gomer? How can we apply them to our own lives?
2. What is the relationship between sin/unfaithfulness and forgiveness/redemption as expressed by the prophet Hosea?
3. What can Hosea tell us about our relationship to God and one another?

Notes

1. Dennis J. McCarthy, S.J. and Roland E. Murphy, O. Carm., "Hosea," *The New Jerome Biblical Commentary.* Eds. Raymond E. Brown, S.S., Joseph A. Fitzmyer, S.J. and Roland E. Murphy, O. Carm., Englewood Cliffs, N.J.: Prentice Hall, Inc, 1990, p. 217.
2. McCarthy and Murphy, p. 220.
3. Hans Walter Wolff. *Hosea.* Trans. Gary Stansell. *Hermeneia—A Critical and Historical Commentary on the Bible,* Paul D. Hanson, Ed., Philadelphia: Fortress Press, 1974, p. 13.

CHAPTER EIGHT

Tobias and Sarah

"Grant that she and I may find mercy and
that we may grow old together."

To find true love, people must often overcome many obstacles. We have seen this truth already in the lives of Ruth and Boaz. We have also seen how the frailty of the human condition or the pressures of outside forces can conspire to block people from finding and expressing their love. For some, past experiences in their families, or of previous relationships, leave them frightened of taking the chance to encounter love. Yet, the ability to overcome such obstacles is one of the characteristics of love. Those with sincere hearts and adventurous spirits find themselves ready to give and receive love in spite of the difficulties and challenges that life throws their way.

The Book of Tobit, a second century B.C. work from the deutero-canonical scriptures (those works accepted by Catholics as Canonical, but called by Protestants the Apocrypha[1]), tells the story of one such love that overcame the impediments that might have caused it to fail. Tobias and Sarah, the young protagonists of this book, find each other only after facing their fears and having faith in each other and in the God who brought them together. In their love they find healing and renewal. They are rewarded for their faithfulness, their righteousness, and their strength of character.[2]

The book of Tobit is, in many ways, a long parable. It is something of an historical folk-tale. Set in the days of the Exile, Tobit reminds the Jews of the post-exilic times of the importance of faithfulness to God in the little things. Tobit, the patriarchal figure in the story, is diligent in performing good deeds, what we might call the "corporal works of mercy." In his own words, Tobit says:

> In the days of Shalmaneser I performed many acts of charity to my kindred, those of my tribe.
> I would give my food to the hungry and my clothing to the naked; and if I saw the dead body of any of my people thrown out behind the wall of Nineveh, I would bury it. (Tob 1:16–17)

Tobit's righteousness, even performed at some personal risk, places him in the company of the Jewish heroes who proceed him in the Scriptures (see especially Judges 6 for an example). The subsequent misfortune that befalls him—his blindness—begs the question: Is it worth it to remain upright in the face of suffering? This question is the subject of the prayer of Tobit (3:1–6), as well as the prayer of Sarah offered at the same time in a distant city (Tob 3:10–15). She, too, faces suffering for no apparent reason, and begs God to help her.

Sarah is a Jewish girl living in Ecbatana in Media (modern Iran). Her tragedy involves her attempts at marriage. Seven times Sarah has been married, and in each instance, on the wedding night, her intended husband has died before they could consummate the marriage. The narrative explains that this misfortune happens through the intervention of a demon, but the words of Sarah's maid betray that many people believe that Sarah has killed them. Distraught, Sarah plans to kill herself, but realizes the despair and disrespect this will cause her father, and because of her love for him she prays instead for God's help. The rest of the Book of Tobit is, in effect, God's answer to these two prayers, and through it, the two families of Tobit and Sarah are brought together.

Tobit, fearing his own impending death, sends his son, Tobias, on a journey to find his fortune. Unknowingly, Tobias chooses the angel Raphael as his traveling companion. God has sent Raphael in answer to the prayers of both Tobit and Sarah; he is to be the instrument of healing in their lives. He helps Tobias find the means of fighting the demon that plagues Sarah. He also provides the salve by which Tobit's blindness is cured. Raphael also instructs Tobias to take Sarah as his wife in fulfillment of the wishes of Tobias's father. Angels are God's messengers and intermediaries in the Scriptures. In this story, Raphael brings God's healing will to Tobit's family, but it is Tobias and Sarah who bring that will to fruition.

Tobias is familiar with Sarah's predicament (Tob 6:14–15), and he is initially afraid. Raphael, however, calms his fears and assures him that God will bring things to a satisfactory conclusion. Tobias has faith, and, like his father, is willing to do the right thing even when it involves personal risk. In fact, knowing Sarah's suffering, Tobias is drawn to her before he even meets her (Tob 6:18).

Tobias and Raphael travel to the house of Sarah's father where Raphael arranges for the wedding of Sarah and Tobias. The story moves quickly now as Tobias insists on marrying Sarah immediately. Sarah's father, Raguel, is honest with Tobias about her history, but Tobias will not be gainsaid. Preparations are therefore begun, and the "marriage contract" is made up "in accordance with the decree in the Book of Moses" (Tob 7:10). Tobias and Sarah are brought together and led to the bridal chamber. Meanwhile, Sarah's father plans for the worst. He even has a grave dug so that Tobias can be buried quickly, but it is unnecessary. Tobias routs the demon by using the instructions given to him by Raphael, and Tobias and Sarah are safe.

Tobias and Sarah then rise from their marriage bed to offer a prayer of thanksgiving to God. This prayer puts forth the book's theology of marriage and shows how Tobias and Sarah stand in the midst of God's plan. They pray:

> So she got up, and they began to pray and implore that they might be kept safe. Tobias began by saying,
> "Blessed are you, O God of our
>   ancestors,
>   and blessed is your name in all
>   generations forever.
> Let the heavens and the whole
>   creation bless you forever.
> You made Adam, and for him
>   you made his wife Eve
> as a helper and support.
>   From the two of them the
>   human race has sprung.
> You said, 'It is not good that the
>   man should be alone;
>   let us make a helper for him
>   like himself.'
> I now am taking this kinswoman
>   of mine,
>   not because of lust,
>   but with sincerity.
> Grant that she and I may find
>   mercy
>   and that we may grow old together."
> And they both said, "Amen, Amen." Then they went to sleep for the night.... (Tob 8:5–9)

Tobias and Sarah see themselves planted firmly within the plan of God for husband and wife. They echo the story of creation in Genesis, and see each other as helpers and as partners through life's unpredictable road. Both had fears as they approached marriage—what couple does not, even if they do not have the special circumstances of Tobias and Sarah? But they realize that together, and with God as a part of their marriage, they can face their fears and overcome them. They recognize in each other that special partner, an equal, who will bring out the best that is in each other. Tobias and Sarah understand the role that God has in their union. God's love brought each of them into existence; God's love brought them together. It is God's love that will sustain their relationship through the good and the bad times of life. This love brings healing and hope to Sarah; it also brings courage and purpose to Tobias.

As God has brought hope and fulfillment to Tobias and Sarah, they bring healing and peace back to Tobit. Tobit, Tobias, and Sarah, all three righteous people, find reward for their righteousness. It has made their paths more difficult, to be sure, but their adversity has strengthened them. God gives them strength, and fortifies their relationship with each other. So the answer to the question asked at the beginning of the book—is it worth being righteous in the face of suffering?—is a resounding *yes*!

The story of Tobias and Sarah is reminiscent of the story of Ruth and Boaz. In both stories the main characters face hardship in their relationships, and they are required to choose between taking an easier path or abiding by their values. Both couples choose the steeper way that follows God's way, and in the end find lasting love. Tobias and Sarah, like Ruth and Boaz, realize how much God is part of their relationship, and in loving each other, they fulfill the purpose of the covenant their love symbolizes.

We live in a time when commitment and love face many obstacles. So many factors can kill love before it has a chance to grow. We carry so much baggage into our relationships. We bring our experiences of growing up in our own families, painful breakups, betrayals of trust, and societal pressures of conforming to an image of the "perfect relationship." These are the demons that plague us. Like Sarah, we can despair of ever finding love. We can sometimes settle for less than we deserve because we are afraid of taking the longer journey. Like Tobias, our fears can blind us to the rewards of perseverance.

Yet, the messengers of God are everywhere. Whether family or friend, they can encourage us, comfort us, and walk with us on our way. With their help, we identify what is important to us and find the strength to adhere to our values. Sticking to our values is its own reward, but it also opens us to find those with similar minds and values. As water seeks its level, human beings seek their soulmates. The still voice that urges us on is the voice of God in our hearts. We are never alone. Together with the "angels" God sends into our lives, we journey toward love. We exorcise the demons that block our path. We remove the blindness that keeps us from seeing God's presence in all our relationships and in all our actions.

Reflection Questions

1. What obstacles do Tobias and Sarah face before they can get married? How do they overcome them?
2. How does God answer the prayers of Tobit and Sarah? What does this say about our prayer expectations?
3. What does the prayer of Tobias and Sarah in Tobit 8:5–9 tell us about God's intentions concerning marriage?

Notes

1. "Canonical" refers to biblical books accepted as inspired by God and belonging to the list of such books; "Apocryphal" refers to books of similar nature to the books of the Bible, but not considered to be inspired. For more detail on the distinction, see Raymond E. Brown, S.S., "Canonicity," in *The New Jerome Biblical Commentary.*

2. Irene Nowell, O.S.B., "Tobit," *The New Jerome Biblical Commentary.* Eds. Raymond E. Brown, S.S., Joseph A. Fitzmyer, S.J. and Roland E. Murphy, O. Carm., Englewood Cliffs, N.J.: Prentice Hall, 1990, p. 568.

CHAPTER NINE

The Song of Solomon

"Arise, my love, my fair one, and come away."

Lovers share a special intimacy that is very difficult to express in words. The language of logic and reason fails in the face of the intensity of their intimacy. Try to explain it, try to prove it, and you will find yourself inarticulate. The language of sexual love is only found in the words of poetry. Poetry takes the risk of being misunderstood and misinterpreted in the hope that it may reveal the depths of its heart.

In this love-poetry the language of love reaches a sublimity that touches our souls. We can perceive the joy, and the playfulness; we can grasp the intensity and the longing; we can sense the depth and the desire that lovers experience in each other. For anyone who has ever been in love, the language of love-poetry strikes a chord deep within. Sexual intimacy and erotic love are also indicators of the love of God, which likewise is hard to express. God created us as sexual beings, and placed within us the desire for such intimacy.

Some might maintain that erotic love is not a fit subject for religious discussion. They believe that there should be a separation between the realm of the spirit and the realm of the flesh. They would be wrong! The clear teaching of the Judeo-Christian tradition is that body and soul are one, united in a singularity that is ultimately inseparable. Both body and soul are created by God. The Scriptures attest to this reality, as does the book to which we now turn—the Song of Solomon.[1]

The Song of Solomon, also known as the Song of Songs, comes to us from the Wisdom tradition of Israel. Ascribed to Solomon, its authorship and date of composition are the subject of scholarly debate. In content it flows in lyrical dialogue between bride and groom extolling the qualities of sexual attraction and *eros*. It is the only book of the Bible where God is named not at all.

The dialogue between bride and groom, the intervention of outsiders (such as the women of the town and the soldiers), the pastoral metaphors, as well as the images of public and private scenes, all unfold in such a way as to extol and highlight the love and the desire of the two main characters. It is quite possible that all or part of this book finds its source in the ancient Israelite rituals of betrothal.[2]

Until quite recently, the overwhelming direction of interpretation for the Song of Solomon was to see it as an allegory. The relationship of lover and beloved was seen as an image of God's love for Israel, as well as Christ's love for the Church. Allegorical interpretation has much to recommend itself. It allows us to access a more personal side of our transcendent God. Marital imagery for the covenant relationship was very popular among the prophets (see especially Hos 2:19–20; Isa 62:5; Ezek 16:6–8). In Revelations 22:17, the Church is described as "the bride." These images show the desire of our God to be intimate with us, and using the powerful language of love and marriage, describes just how close we can be with our God. The Lord is a person with whom we can have a personal relationship. The Song of Songs is an apt description of that relationship, and of the image of God as love.

Yet, throughout the centuries, and more so in recent scholarship, the literal understanding of the Song of Solomon as an erotic love-poem is upheld. Following from the interpretation of Genesis 2, described above, Song of Songs continues the portrait of human love, and specifically sexual love, in the positive light of God's good and continuing creation. Sexual love, properly seen, is good in its own right and worthy of inclusion in the canon of Scripture.

In fact, the literal interpretation of the Song of Solomon as a poem or series of poems about marital love allows us entry into the allegorical. Before we can talk about the intimate love of God for humanity, we first have to understand our capacity for showing and receiving love. We have to experience and express our experience of intimacy to have a language that we understand. So let us look at the language of *eros* expressed in Song of Songs so that we can begin to understand the delight God takes in human love.

Before we look at the Song itself, we need to put it into the contest of the culture in which it was written. Specifically, we have to examine the difference between Canaanite and Israelite views of the role of sex in the community. The Canaanites were farmers. Their concern was for the fertility of their fields, as well as their community. They saw an intrinsic link between the cycle of seasons and the sexual act. Sex and eroticism were expressions of the fertility of the whole community. It was believed that the sexual act mirrored the sexual acts of the gods, which the Canaanites believed ensured the fruitfulness of their fields and the growth of their crops. This belief led to the rise of ritual prostitution in Canaanite religious worship. Sex became part of temple ritual and, in this sense, separated from the realm of love and human relationships.[3]

When the nomadic Hebrew tribes came into Canaan after the Exodus and began to settle and become farmers themselves, they were tempted to follow Canaanite rituals. After all, they had been shepherds, so what did they know about farming? If those who were farmers for generations felt that this link between sex and fertility worked, who were they to argue? Throughout the period of the Judges, the monarchy, and the divided kingdom, this temptation to follow the Canaanite fertility rituals plagued Israel. The prophets fought against it, and continued to reject the divinization of sexuality that was both a form of idolatry and a reduction of sexuality to merely an act that did not involve true relationship between human beings. Human love and sexuality are good, but only within the proper context. While sex and procreation are a participation in the creative power of God, the prophets taught that sexual activity is not a cause of creation or fertility, nor does it cause the fruitfulness of the land. Erotic love and sex are only good when they express the *Covenant relationship*. Commitment, mutuality, and faithfulness are the hallmarks of the healthy sexuality to which the people of Israel were called.

When seen in this light, the message of the Song of Solomon takes on a new significance. The playfulness and delight that the lovers take in each other are expressions of a serious insight. Sex and sexuality are part of the plan of God for human beings; it is a plan that involves relationship between the lovers. It is not just participation in a cosmic fertility cycle. Sex and *eros*, properly seen, are good in themselves for what they bring to humankind—a relationship based on *love*.

Because the Song is placed within this positive view of sexuality, it is able to be quite frank in its expressions. The bride and bridegroom describe their love and longing for one another in expressive images that mince no words. We know of the pride they take in themselves and the delight they take in each other's bodies. They use pastoral language of the vineyard, flock, and farm to paint word pictures that, even today in our urbanized and technological society, touch our imaginations. We know the joy of a lover's kiss (1:2), the thrill of hearing the beloved's voice (2:8), and the special light that shines in a partner's eyes only for ourselves (4:1). We also know the pain of separation (6:1), whether enforced by outside considerations, or chosen through personal circumstances.

The Song of Songs presents these elements in a most appealing light. There is nothing demeaning or degrading in this presentation of sexual language. There is no harassment or abuse here. Bride and groom are equal in their desire, delight, and devotion. Their attraction is mutual, and their participation in love based on the highest motives. This is not a poem about lust; it is a song of life-giving love. It recognizes that true love—the prerequisite for sexual love—is difficult, and it admits that love is one of the most powerful of human motivations. "Love is strong as death" (8:6). We know that death is one thing stronger than human beings, since we all succumb to it, but love is at least the equal of death, and quite possibly stronger since it can not be "quenched" or "drowned." Nor is it something that can be bought; only freely given.

This love, then, seen so openly in its sexual and erotic forms, is not the emotion of being in love that we so often equate with the word. These feelings are the starting point that leads lovers deeper into their relationship. Lovers choose one another, and continue to do so throughout their whole lives. This choosing, over and over, is the heart of marital love. It is the center of the marriage ceremony, which sacramentalizes love, even as it wraps it in romantic trappings. A man and a woman say, "I choose you, for better *and* for worse, for richer *and* for poorer, in sickness *and* in health, for the rest of my life." There is no multiple choice in these vows. Husband and wife choose the whole package.

Of course, the lived reality of this ideal is never quite as simple. Other factors intrude into the lives of the couple. Even within the Song, the interventions of the townswomen (5:9;

6:1) and the soldiers (3:3; 5:7) foreshadow conflict. Sexual, erotic love, good in itself, is not an end in itself. Eroticism, promiscuity, and unfaithfulness are also realities in the world of love. Selfishness and suspicion can poison the joy with which so many lovers start their lives. We sing the Song of Solomon to a broken world, yet what inspiration this song can give!

The Song of Songs highlights the basic goodness of sexual love and intimacy. In its proper perspective, this love brings together a married couple and helps them find in each other the complementarity intended by the Creator from the beginning. In their sexual loving, they find their life-giving potential, first to each other, and then to the children their love may beget. Many people do not experience love this way, but for those who do, only one word comes to mind to describe it—holy. Because of this sense of holiness, the church blesses marriages; it recognizes this basic truth about human sexual love: it is a sign of God's redemptive love.

And so, we are now back to the allegorical interpretation from which we began. Human loving is symbol of God's loving. The elements we see in the Song of Solomon not only tell us how we should love each other, but they tell us how God loves us—with passion, with joy, with playfulness—and as strong as death.

Reflection Questions

1. How can *eros* and marital imagery explain our relationship with God?
2. How do our intimate relationships with spouse, family and friends help us experience the love of God?
3. What is the difference between contemporary society's view of sexuality, and the Judeo-Christian view expressed in the Song of Solomon?

Notes

1. Morris, *Testament of Love—A Study of Love in the Bible*, p. 51.
2. Roland E. Murphy, O. Carm. *The Song of Songs*. Hermeneia —A Critical and Historical Commentary on the Bible. Ed. S. Dean McBride, Jr., Minneapolis: Fortress Press, 1990, pp. 98–99.
3. Marvin H. Pope. *The Song of Songs*. The Anchor Bible. Garden City: Doubleday & Company, 1977, pp. 202–203; Roland E. Murphy, O. Carm., "Canticle of Canticles," *The New Jerome Biblical Commentary*. Eds. Raymond E. Brown, S.S., Joseph A. Fitzmyer, S.J. and Roland E. Murphy, O. Carm, Englewood Cliffs, N.J.: Prentice Hall, 1990, p. 463.

CHAPTER TEN

Joseph and Mary

Joseph was a righteous man.

In the previous chapter on the Song of Solomon, we discussed how true love, which expresses itself through sexual love, is based on choice—a decision to love one person and commit oneself to that person, in the words of the wedding vows, "for better or worse." This choice is not a one-time decision. In a relationship of love, be it married love, friendship, or family, we base our decisions on that love. We can see in these choices the depths of a person's love. People who make a choice to pass up a promotion at work because it would uproot their families; people who change their lifestyle to take care of ailing loved ones; people who remain faithful day after day to their spouses; people who give freely of their time and talent for the sake of their children—these people continuously make loving decisions that show forth the lived reality of love.

In the Bible, we see many examples of people who make choices for love. Possibly, one of the best examples is found in the Infancy Narratives of Matthew's Gospel. Here we are presented with Joseph, a devout Jewish man who is drawn into the mystery of God's saving plan. Matthew's Gospel seems to tell the story of Jesus' birth from Joseph's perspective, and in many ways, he is the main character in the first two chapters of this

Gospel. The decisions and choices he makes in the early years of Jesus' life show us the loving character of this man.

Before we look in more detail at Joseph's role in the Infancy Stories, I want to mention Mary. By choosing to look at Joseph first, I in no way want to say that Mary did not make loving choices. In the next chapter, we will look at Mary's role (as expressed in Luke's Gospel). Mary takes a more passive role in Matthew's Infancy Narratives and, in this chapter, only from the literary point of view. Certainly, Mary's "yes" to the angel was an example of a loving decision and an expression of her faith in the loving plan of God. For simplicity's sake, we will examine Joseph's role as recorded by Matthew before looking at Mary's response in this two-part love story.

First, let us say a word about Infancy Narratives themselves.[1] The stories recounted in Matthew 1 and 2 and Luke 1 and 2 are not the Christmas story. Christmas as a Church celebration of the birth of Jesus comes rather later than the formation of the Gospels, not until the third century A.D. Many of our traditions about Christmas come from legend or attempts to harmonize the different stories in Matthew and Luke. Neither of these sacred authors, however, were much interested in recounting the birth of Jesus for its own sake. The authors intended these sections of the gospels to introduce their proclamations of the Good News. They are more than introductions or prologues, however, for they each make important *theological* statements about who Jesus is. Matthew and Luke also use them to refute criticism leveled at Jesus about his origins during the Lord's own lifetime and in the experience of the early Church.

So what is the point of these stories in Matthew and Luke? The sacred authors want to situate the life, actions, death, and resurrection of Jesus within a framework. Who is this person the gospels call Christ? From the very announcement of his birth, he was the fulfillment of God's promise of salvation. Joseph and

Mary have a part to play in this plan, and are road signs in the Infancy Narratives that point out Jesus' specialness. Long before John the Baptist cries, "prepare the way of the Lord, make his paths straight," (Mark 1:3), Joseph and Mary prepare for the Messiah's mission by the loving way they care for Jesus.

Matthew begins his account of the birth of Jesus Christ with a list of Jesus' forebears. This genealogy was written in the tradition of the Hebrew Scriptures from whom Matthew derives a fair amount of his material. The study of Matthew's genealogy for Christ and its comparison to Luke's version is, in itself, a fascinating endeavor.[2] Suffice it to say for our purposes that Matthew wants to make two clear theological statements about the human origins of the Messiah. First, that Jesus is a descendant of Abraham—the father not only of the Hebrew people, but the source of God's covenant with humanity—and second, that Jesus is the descendant of David—through whom the promised Messiah was to come. Joseph's role in relation to Jesus is important in this second assertion of Jesus' ancestry because Jesus had to be seen as a *legal* descendant of David, and legality came through the father of a child. Joseph is described in Matthew 1:20 as "son of David." His role, traditionally ascribed as Jesus' *foster father,* should more correctly (and importantly) be termed *legal father.* The decisions Joseph makes concerning Mary and Jesus play a significant part in establishing Jesus' ties to the lineage of the promised Messiah.[3]

There are four decisions that Joseph makes in the opening chapters of Matthew's Gospel that show his character and his love. The first two deal with Mary, the second two with the Holy Family as a whole. Matthew describes the situation thus:

> When his [Jesus'] mother had been engaged to Joseph, but before they lived together, she was found to be with child from the Holy Spirit. (Matt 1:18)

Jewish marriage customs in the first century had two parts. First, there was a formal engagement or betrothal. This ceremony was a legally binding exchange of vows that had the same impact as our contemporary wedding ceremony. Second, sometime later, the betrothed couple would take up residence together and live thenceforth as husband and wife.[4] Matthew presupposes that the first part of this twofold tradition had taken place before the events he narrates. Mary and Joseph have publicly made their betrothal promises to one another. Further, Matthew explicitly says that they had *not* begun to live together. That Mary is with child "of the Holy Spirit" is something only the readers of the gospel know, not Joseph. Joseph only knows that he and Mary have not had sexual relations, and can only presume that she has been unfaithful to him. He would be perfectly within his rights to expose her publicly to disgrace as an adulteress and have her stoned to death. His decision, then, portrays the depth of compassion in this man.

> Her husband Joseph, being a righteous man and unwilling to expose her to public disgrace, planned to dismiss her quietly. (Matt 1:19)

Joseph is described as a righteous man. Other translations call him "upright" and "just." The Jewish law concerning adultery was clear, but Joseph seems unwilling to follow it. How then are we to understand his righteousness in relation to the law?

Joseph loved Mary. There is no reason to believe otherwise. The entire story of his actions toward her and Jesus in Matthew 1 and 2 show this love to be true. Perhaps Joseph realized in his heart what Jesus would later teach, that the law—justice—had to be tempered with mercy (Matt 23:23). It seems that Joseph's righteousness came not from literal observance of the law, but from his compassion.[5] He cannot see Mary hurt, and so, out of love, he decides to dismiss or divorce her privately and quietly. What this means we are not sure, but it was somehow conceived to prevent Mary from being communally tried as an adulteress, or to give her the opportunity to go elsewhere and "start over."

Then, however, Joseph has an experience that makes him change his mind. In a scene reminiscent of the patriarchs (particularly Jacob in Gen 28:10–17) Joseph goes to sleep and has a revelatory dream. In chapter four we saw how dreams are an important way of representing divine communication. Here in Matthew 1 and 2, dreams and angels keep Joseph very, very busy. The angelic message in Matthew 1:20–23 follows a set pattern. He is told not to fear, then he is told how God is acting in the mysterious things that are happening. Finally, he is told what to do. "Do not be afraid," the angel says. God moves to remove fear. Love conquers fear. Do not be afraid to follow love.

The angel relates to Joseph that the child growing in Mary's womb is of the Holy Spirit. Mary has not been unfaithful; rather, she has been extremely faithful in doing God's will, and Joseph is now called to be part of the divine plan of salvation. Would God choose anyone but the righteous, compassionate, and loving man that Joseph is to bring that plan to fruition?

Besides assuring Joseph that he should have no fear and take Mary home as his wife, the angel says two other important things. He calls Joseph "Son of David," recalling the genealogy that opens the gospel. This Messiah is of the house of David. The angel also tells Joseph to name the child Jesus. Joseph is not the natural father of the child, but by naming him, Joseph becomes the legal father, and Jesus becomes his legal heir, and thereby a descendant of David. Thus the prophecy that the Messiah would be from the house and lineage of David is fulfilled. Further, the bond between Joseph and Jesus becomes that of father and son, because by naming him, Joseph accepts Jesus as his own.

Waking from his dream, Joseph promptly does as the angel directed him. This action is the second loving decision of Joseph, and it could not have been without consequence. Joseph and Mary live in a small town. People would know that there was some irregularity in this relationship and in the child's conception. Joseph, out of love for God and for Mary, takes responsibility for her and her unborn child despite all the gossip and turmoil it might cause. Here again we see Joseph's righteousness. Knowing that taking Mary as his wife is the right thing to do, Joseph does it, no matter the cost. Love gives him the strength to do so.

Interestingly, Jesus' birth is not really recounted in Matthew's Gospel. We are told only that Mary bore a son and Joseph named him Jesus. The second chapter of Matthew goes on to give us the reactions to this birth. The stories of the Magi and of King Herod are well known, and much can be said about their roles in the Infancy Narrative. For our purposes, the evil actions of Herod act as a foil for the loving actions of Joseph.

Once again, Joseph is told in a dream what he is to do. Herod is seeking the child to do harm to him. It is no longer safe for Joseph and his family in Bethlehem. So Joseph takes his wife and young child (who may have been as old as two; see Matt 2:16) and goes to Egypt. Joseph decides to lead his family into the *diaspora,* the scattering of the Jewish people outside the Promised Land. We do not know where in Egypt the Holy Family settled, nor how long they stayed there. Certainly such a trip would have been a hardship. It is always difficult to leave behind what is familiar. Joseph would have faced many difficult questions. Could he find work to support his family? Where would they live? How could they remain faithful to their Jewish heritage in a foreign land? Despite these questions, Joseph does not hesitate. It seems from the wording of Matthew 2:14 that he left the very same night that he was warned in the dream, and took his family to safety. We might ask what other choice he had, but still, his actions are the actions that come from love.

Now imagine that Joseph has settled himself and his little family in Egypt. He probably found one of the many Jewish communities in Egypt and began to establish himself and his household. He found work, made friends, and settled into the routines of local life. Again, however, those pesky angels reveal to him that Herod is dead, and it is time for him to bring the child and his mother back to the Promised Land. Joseph is now faced with another decision.

Joseph's decision here is twofold. First, he must leave behind the work and effort he has accomplished to situate himself in Egypt. Returning home to Palestine would not have been as difficult as leaving in the first place, but it involved uprooting his family, making a long journey, probably on foot, with a young child, and the disruption of his newly founded life in Egypt. For many people the mere inconveniences of such a trip would have deterred them. Not so Joseph! Once more we see how Joseph responds immediately to the angel's command. Regardless of Joseph's intuition about Jesus' future career as "savior," he must have also believed that it was better to raise Jesus as a good Jew in the Jewish homeland.

The second part of this decision for Joseph concerned where to go. Matthew assumes that Bethlehem was Joseph and Mary's hometown. There is no indication in Matthew's Gospel that Joseph had previously been a resident of Nazareth. His decision to settle in Galilee rather than return to Judea was based on his concern for his family. Herod's son, Archelaus, was named tetrarch of Judea, and his reputation for cruelty was worse than his father Herod's. Joseph brings his family to

Galilee and Nazareth to ensure their safety. Of course, this new settlement means that again he would have to reestablish himself. He had to find a home, a job, and gain a reputation as a good and honest worker. Joseph's decision to settle in Nazareth shows his loving and self-sacrificing nature.

It is not without reason that Joseph is called the patron and protector of families. His actions show us a model of compassion, openness, faith and self-sacrifice. Contrast him with the character of Jacob from Genesis. Jacob is always ready to think of himself first, to wheel and deal and find a way out of doing the right thing. Joseph shows by his actions what love is. He puts the safety of Mary and Jesus first, and he follows what his faith tells him is right. It is not surprising that Joseph has a family that loves him in return. Loving decisions, lovingly made, and even hard to take, bring back a return of love that is often unexpected.

At the heart of these decisions is Joseph's ability to see and respond to the needs of others. Love is other-centered. So much of what passes for love today is selfish. It is meant to satisfy personal needs and demands. Affection and sexual attraction are often mistaken for love because they make one *feel* good, but this feeling is illusory and, in the end, decisions based on them can degrade and hurt us. To give of ourselves and subsume our needs for the needs of another, on the other hand, can paradoxically satisfy our needs, too. I am not talking here about what has been termed "codependency." Certainly, the conscious or unconscious *negation* of my own needs so as to hold on to another or attach myself to him or her is unhealthy. I, as an individual person, can disappear in this type of relationship. Joseph's self-denial does not cause his personality to disappear. It makes him stronger, as all truly loving decisions make us stronger. Truly loving decisions weigh our own needs against the needs of another so as to make the best decision for both. If it is true that children grow up to be like their parents, then one can wonder whether Jesus grew up to be the loving and self-sacrificing savior because of what he learned, in part, from Joseph.

Reflection Questions

1. How do Joseph's decisions in chapters one and two of Matthew show his love for God, for Mary, and for Jesus?
2. What can we learn from Joseph about justice and righteousness?
3. What is the connection between self-sacrifice and love as seen in the gospel portrait of Joseph?

Notes

1. For a summary of contemporary scholarship on Infancy Narratives, see: Raymond E. Brown. *The Birth of the Messiah*. New Updated Edition, New York: Doubleday, 1993, pp. 25–41; Benedict Viviano, "The Gospel According to Matthew," *The New Jerome Biblical Commentary*. Eds. Raymond E. Brown, S.S., Joseph A. Fitzmyer, S.J. and Roland E. Murphy, O. Carm., Englewood Cliffs, N.J.: Prentice-Hall, 1990, pp. 634–635.
2. See: Brown, *Birth*, pp. 57–95.
3. Krister Stendahl, "*Quis et unde?* An Analysis of Matthew 1–2," in *The Interpretation of Matthew*. Ed. Graham Stanton. Issues in Religion and Theology 3, Philadelphia: Fortress Press, 1983, p. 61.
4. Brown, *The Birth of the Messiah*, pp. 123–124. And Cohen-Sherbok, *A Popular Dictionary of Judaism,* pp. 108–109.
5. Eduard Schweizer. *The Good News According to Matthew*. Trans. David E. Green, Atlanta: John Knox Press, 1975, pp. 30–31.

CHAPTER ELEVEN

Mary and Joseph

"Here am I, the servant of the Lord."

If marriage is, indeed, a partnership, then we have only examined half of the story. The love story of Joseph and Mary, like that of Ruth and Boaz, and Tobias and Sarah, is the story of *two* people of faith whose trust in God helped them to be loving people. Mary, too, made loving decisions, and loving actions fill her life. She was wife and mother, and, to be sure, these roles inspired her to loving deeds. But Mary is also a disciple, and as a disciple showed her love for God by the things she said and did.

As Matthew's Gospel highlighted Joseph's role in Jesus' early life, the Infancy Narratives in the Gospel of Luke center on Mary. Here we witness the annunciation, the visitation, and the nativity. In each episode, we see how Mary responded lovingly to the Word of God by her own words and her actions.

Luke, like Matthew, uses the vehicle of Infancy Stories to make important *theological* assertions about Jesus. Themes that are significant throughout the gospel are woven all through the first two chapters of Luke. While all the stories of this section are ways of presenting Jesus and his message to the world, Mary is the central character here, and her actions and attitudes set the tone for all Christians in responding to the Lord. It goes without saying that love underlies such responses, and Mary's loving character shows itself very clearly.[1]

We saw in Matthew's Gospel how Joseph's loving decisions led him to perform loving deeds. In Luke, it is Mary's trusting love of God and the Word of God that inspired her to do loving things. She is contrasted to Zechariah, the father of John the Baptist, who is unable to put his faith in God's word, and so is, initially, silenced and moved to the background of the story (Luke 1:20). Mary's trust allows her to give voice to her relationship with God and move to the center of the action. This point is made not to indicate that Zechariah is unloving, but to highlight the source of Mary's loving deeds. They flow from a fundamental trust in the love of God.

We first see Mary at the scene known as the annunciation (Luke 1:26–38). Here, following the pattern of birth announcements in the Hebrew Scriptures (see: Gen 18:9–15; Judg 13:2–18; 1 Sam 1:9–18), Mary is informed of the plan of God, and asked to be part of it. Her story parallels the annunciation of John the Baptist's birth to Zechariah in Luke 1:5–24. The announcement to Mary, however, has some important differences that Luke uses to highlight the difference between John and Jesus. From the very beginning of the Gospel, Luke wants his readers to know that the Messiah is unique.

> In the sixth month the angel Gabriel was sent by God to a town in Galilee called Nazareth, to a virgin engaged to a man whose name was Joseph, of the house of David. The virgin's name was Mary. And he came to her and said, "Greetings, favored one! The Lord is with you." But she was much perplexed by his words and pondered what sort of greeting this might be. The angel said to her, "Do not be afraid, Mary, for you have found favor with God. And now, you will conceive in your womb and bear a son, and you will name him Jesus. He will

be great, and will be called the Son of the Most High, and the Lord God will give to him the throne of his ancestor David. He will reign over the house of Jacob forever, and of his kingdom there will be no end." (Luke 1:26–33)

The "sixth month" refers to the conception of John the Baptist by Elizabeth and Zechariah. Luke connects the mission of Jesus and John the Baptist by connecting their lives from the very beginning. The angelic greeting is similar to other birth announcements as the angel declares, "Do not be afraid." The Word of God that Mary is about to hear will be challenging and difficult, but it is not a cause for fear. God's love, the source of all love, takes away fear and makes room for loving responses.

The angel announces the message of God's love as Gabriel tells Mary that she is "favored," that is, chosen to be the mother of the Messiah. This messiah is to be both Son of God and son of David (see parallel passage in Matt 1:20). Unlike David, though, who died and whose dynasty eventually ended, this king will reign forever. The child to be born to Mary will be unlike Isaac, Samson, Samuel, or even John the Baptist (whose births were likewise preannounced). The love that Mary is asked to show by becoming the mother of Jesus is far beyond that asked of her biblical forebears. Isaac, Samson, Samuel, and John the Baptist all had ministries to perform, but Mary is being asked to enter into a mystery heretofore unknown. Her next words show that this birth announcement is very different from the ones of her religious heritage.

Mary said to the angel, "How can this be, since I am a virgin?" The angel said to her, "The Holy Spirit will come upon you, and the power of the Most High will over-shadow you; therefore the child to be born will be holy; he will be called Son of God. And now, your relative

Elizabeth in her old age has also conceived a son; and this is the sixth month for her who was said to be barren. For nothing will be impossible with God." (Luke 1:34–37)

When faced with a similar announcement, Zechariah responded with skepticism and doubt (Luke 1:18). Mary's question here is more practical. Zechariah and Elizabeth are a married couple, and even though beyond the normal age for childbearing, the conception of John the Baptist still takes place through natural means. Luke makes it very clear (as does Matthew) that Mary and Joseph are betrothed but not yet living together as husband and wife. In first century Judaism, the betrothal ceremony was a binding one. It sealed the commitment of the two individuals involved as completely as does our wedding ceremony today. There was, however, a lapse in time of up to a year between the formal betrothal and the time when the couple began to live together.[2] Mary and Joseph are in this in-between time. Mary is a virgin, and is being asked to become a mother in a mysterious and unique way. Her question is not doubt; it is a desire to understand the mystery. Luke wants to make absolutely certain that Jesus' conception, while similar in circumstance to that of Isaac, Samson, Samuel, and John (i.e., it responds to the need of the people for a savior or prophet), is achieved only through the power of God. Mary conceives not by natural means, but through the overshadowing of the Holy Spirit. Her child will be "Son of God" in a way different from any other person in Jewish history. In this child, God is doing something new, for "nothing will be impossible for God" (Luke 1:37).

Mary's response shows her as a loving disciple. She says, "Here am I, the servant of the Lord, let it be with me according to your word" (Luke 1:38). Mary's acquiescence to

Gabriel's request is not just a "yes" to doing God's will. It is more than an act of faith; it is an act of trust and love for Joseph as well. Mary is no fool. She knows the implications in her society for being pregnant before she had come to live with her husband. As we saw in Matthew, if Joseph had not believed in her, if he had chosen to expose her as an adulteress, then Mary would have faced execution. We really know nothing about the relationship between Joseph and Mary up to this point. Was their marriage an arranged affair? While it is improbable that in a small town they would not have known each other, the mores of first century Jewish life would have precluded much interaction or any private time at all. Yet, Mary makes a choice to do God's will, and shows trust in Joseph's character. Such trust is the foundation of love. The subsequent actions of Mary and Joseph as a couple, and as parents, demonstrate that this foundation was well built upon in their relationship with one another and with Jesus.

Mary's love leads her immediately into action. As part of her experience with the angel, Mary is informed about Elizabeth, her relative, who is already six months pregnant with John the Baptist. So "Mary set out and went in haste...where she entered the house of Zechariah and greeted Elizabeth" (Luke 1:39–40). This scene in the gospel, known to us as the visitation, brings onto the stage the two great protagonists of Luke's Infancy Story. Elizabeth, the mother of John the Baptist, represents the prophetic past, while Mary, the mother of Jesus, represents the new age of salvation.

The interaction between Mary and Elizabeth allows them both to give voice to their experience of God. Both Mary and Elizabeth have encountered God's power. Mary now expresses how the Lord is her savior, as God has always been for those in need. In the Magnificat, Mary's song of praise, she sings of God as one who loves, and whose love reverses the injustices of the sinful world.

Luke tells us that Mary stayed with Elizabeth "about three months" (Luke 1:56). Chronologically, this statement would have Mary leaving just as John was born, when Elizabeth would need her most—a most uncharacteristic action. We have to remember that Luke, the author and the artist, needed to have Mary out of the picture for the birth of John the Baptist for thematic purposes. John's birth scene emphasized his mission and role, and could not be overshadowed by the presence of the messiah's mother. Mary's haste to go to Elizabeth is the sign of her compassion and loving response.

After recounting the birth of John the Baptist and the miraculous events surrounding it (Luke 1:57–80), the sacred author then recounts the familiar story of Jesus' birth. Luke's story is very different from Matthew's version. Matthew mentions nothing about a census, the long trip from Nazareth to Bethlehem, the manger, the shepherds, or the angels. The story of the nativity is Luke the storyteller at his best. He shows conflict, mystery, and revelation. He captures the drama of the event, and makes definite statements about the religious significance of the birth of this child.

The setting in which Luke situates the scene of Jesus' birth—namely, the census, the trip to Bethlehem, and the lack of lodging for the young couple in their time of need—tend to foreshadow the life and ministry of Jesus. He was born, lived, and died at the time of Roman ascendancy in the Western world. It framed his mission and affected the way his word was presented to society. His life and mission were in fulfillment of ancient prophecy (see Mic 5:2). Finally, Jesus was born, not to privilege and power, but to poverty and powerlessness. Later in Luke, Jesus will say, "Foxes have holes, and birds of the air have nests, but the Son of Man has nowhere to lay his head"

(Luke 9:58). Jesus was born as he lived, a pilgrim in this world. Mary, Jesus' mother and his disciple, follows closely in her life, too. She and Joseph are also pilgrims as they seek to do God's will.

As in Matthew, the actual birth scene of Jesus is given short shrift. It is noted:

> While they were there, the time came for her to deliver her child. And she gave birth to her firstborn son and wrapped him in bands of cloth, and laid him in a manger, because there was no place for them in the inn. (Luke 2:6–7)

Certainly there is a little more information here than in Matthew 1:25, but hardly enough to know what really happened. Legend has filled in the details over the centuries, but the actual Scriptures are more concerned with reactions to the Savior's birth than with the actual occurrence. The humble beginnings of Jesus' life are recounted, well, humbly. We are told only enough information to know that it happened, and that Mary took loving care of her infant son. Swaddling a child in bands of cloth was seen as a sign of parental care (see Wis 7:4 and Ezek 16:4). Mary, a new mother, takes care of her baby as lovingly as any new young mother would. She and Joseph greeted the miracle of Jesus' birth in the same way as any parents would: with joy, apprehension, and loving care.

The events that follow the birth of Jesus, that is, the announcement to the shepherds, their visit, and their return praising God for all they had seen and heard, all serve as sources for Mary's reflection. Along with the annunciation and the visitation, the episodes that surround Jesus' birth cause Mary to consider the mysterious ways of God. As any mother would, Mary holds the memories of her child's birth dear. Yet, she is also aware that they have impact beyond her ken. She treasures the memories and dreams hope-filled dreams about his future. Mary is, however, not only Jesus' mother; Luke presents her as Jesus' disciple as well. As she ponders his birth, she will also do so as he grows (Luke 2:51), and during his ministry. This pondering leads Mary to reflect on God's word, and to respond in loving ways. Because Mary is able to contemplate the loving deeds that God shows forth in her son's life, death, and resurrection, she is at the center of the community formed in his name (see Acts 1:14).

From the very early days of the church, devotion to Mary the mother of God has flourished. She is seen as the model believer, the faithful servant and *Theotokos,* the "God-bearer." Her words in the early chapters of Luke's Gospel frame the loving response of all Christians. She perceives God's word working in her life, and gives voice to the hope of God's power permeating the world. Mary responds to this word with deeds of love for Elizabeth, for Joseph, and for her child, Jesus. She says "yes" to God's plan of salvation, even when it involves risk. She hurries to bring the love she has felt to her relative Elizabeth. She trusts in Joseph's love and faithfulness. She welcomes her child in love, even in the difficult circumstances of his birth. She ponders these events so that she may continue to respond in loving ways.

Mary is a mother, and so becomes a model for all mothers. She embodies that special type of love that is called "maternal." It is a self-sacrificing love. A love that is willing to give without counting cost, and one that puts the needs of the child before any personal needs. It is a love that has played itself out in countless families over and over through generations. We see it in the gentle picture of a mother cooing over her infant, and in the concern and worry of a mother's love for her adult child. It is a love that knows when to let go, without letting go of the special connection of mother and child. It is a love that knows grief and joy.

Mary is also a wife. We do not know the details of the home life of Joseph and Mary. The Scriptures are silent about the childhood of Jesus (except for the incident when he was twelve, as recounted in Luke 2:40–52). The Scriptures do give us a picture of Jesus as an adult, however. He was a gentle, compassionate, and loving man. He reached out to those in need. He had a special place in his heart for children. He sacrificed his life for the sake of his love. If children grow up to be like their parents, then Mary and Joseph must have been wonderful ones indeed.

Reflection Questions

1. What role do faith and trust play in loving relationships?
2. How does Mary put love into action with Elizabeth and the infant Jesus? What do these actions imply about our own loving relationships?
3. What does Mary's role as a mother in Luke's Gospel teach us about love and about God?

Notes

1. Brown, *The Birth of the Messiah,* pp. 235–255.
2. See note no. 4 in previous chapter.

CHAPTER TWELVE

Jesus and Mary Magdalene

"I have seen the Lord."

The loving relationship of Joseph and Mary taught Jesus to be a loving person. From the example of Joseph, righteous and just, willing to sacrifice for the sake of his loved ones, and from the example of Mary, humble and loving, open to the prompting of the Spirit, Jesus learned to be just, self-sacrificing, humble, and open. When he began his public ministry, Jesus attracted loving people into the circle of his followers. When we examine some of these relationships, we see the way love changed them and made them more than followers of Jesus— they became his closest friends.

One of the loving relationships in Jesus' life was with Mary of Magdala. All four gospels mention her, especially in relation to the "empty tomb" stories. The gospels show her as a woman who deeply loved Jesus, and her love allowed her to be the first to see him after the resurrection. But just who is Mary Magdalene? What kind of relationship did she have with Jesus?

Tradition has not always been fair to Mary Magdalene. She has been described as a reformed sinner, a harlot. The Apocryphal writings (those early writings about Jesus often supposed to be from the hands of the disciples but never accepted into the Canonical Scriptures) saw her as a rival to Peter in church leadership. The later Middle Ages developed quite a cult of following for Mary of Magdala, but many of the devotions to her were based on legend, not fact. We are concerned here only with what the gospels have to say about her, and particularly the portrait of her presented in the Gospel of John.[1]

Magdala was a Galilean fishing village on the shore of the Sea of Galilee.[2] It is southwest of Capernaum and Bethsaida. The gospels never mention that Jesus went there, nor is there any mention made of it except in relation to Mary's origin. Since Mary was a very common name, the toponymic *Magdalene* is used universally in all four gospels to indicate which Mary. With the exception of Luke, Mary Magdalene is first mentioned in the Passion Narrative. Mark (and depending on him, Matthew) tells us that Mary was one of a group of women from Galilee who followed Jesus, and provided for him out of their means (Mark 15:40–41; Matt 27:55–56). Luke tells us that these women who, along with the twelve, followed Jesus had been "cured of evil spirits and infirmities" (Luke 8:1–3). Mary Magdalene, whose name always heads the list, was said to have been cured "of seven demons."

In ancient Israel, demons were thought to be the cause of all sickness, and the phrase "seven demons" would indicate a serious or possibly recurring ailment that Jesus cured. It in no way implies a moral problem in Mary. Later attempts to harmonize the stories of Mary of Magdala, Mary of Bethany (sister of Martha and Lazarus), and the unnamed sinful woman of Luke 7:36–50 have led to the conclusion that Mary Magdalene was a repentant sinner, perhaps a public sinner whose reputation was well known. There is, however no scriptural evidence to indicate that these three women should be viewed as the same person.[3]

Whoever she might be, or whatever her background, Mary of Magdala left her home to follow Jesus from Galilee to

Jerusalem. It is in Jerusalem, at the foot of the cross and at the empty tomb, that we begin to see what kind of love Mary had for Jesus, and how the resurrection changed that love relationship.

The Gospel of Mark, the earliest of the written gospels, recounts that Mary Magdalene, along with some other women who had come from Galilee, was present at the crucifixion, looking on at a distance from the cross. They seem to be the only followers of Jesus who have at least come to witness the end. They also see where Jesus is buried and come "very early on the first day of the week" (Mark 16:2) to anoint the body of Jesus. Worried about the large stone that sealed his tomb, they were surprised to see that it was already rolled back. Mark describes the tomb as empty, except for a "young man dressed in a white robe" (16:5) who announces the resurrection and tells the women to return to the disciples and tell them. Stricken with terror, the women leave and tell no one.

Mark's presentation is the least flattering to Mary and the women followers, but it is also the least flattering to the disciples as a whole. The women's silence regarding the empty tomb is part of a larger leitmotif in Mark about the misunderstanding of Jesus by his closest followers. Mary Magdalene and her companions were willing to follow Jesus to the cross, but they lacked resurrection faith—the faith that Mark calls his community to have in the face of hardship and persecution.

Matthew's presentation of this story depends largely on Mark, but Matthew adds some other details that fill out our portrait of Mary. In Matthew's version, Mary Magdalene and another woman named Mary visit the tomb "as the first day of the week was dawning" (Matt 28:1). They witness an earthquake and see an angel come and roll back the stone. Matthew adds these apocalyptic touches to emphasize that with the death and resurrection of Jesus, the world has entered a new and final age. In effect, the world has ended, and the reign of God has begun. Matthew describes the women running to tell the disciples the news and actually meeting the risen Lord on the way, thus being the first of Jesus' followers to witness an appearance of Jesus after the resurrection.

Luke seems to strike a middle ground between Mark's account and Matthew's. Mary Magdalene and the women indeed come to the tomb early on Sunday morning to find the stone rolled back and "two men in dazzling clothes" (Luke 24:4) present. These men ask the question, "Why do you seek the living among the dead?" The women go immediately to tell the disciples, who do not believe them. Peter, however, runs to the tomb and sees that the report of Mary and the other women is true. As yet, though, neither Peter nor any of Jesus' followers seems to have grasped the full meaning of the empty tomb.

The synoptic accounts all agree that Mary Magdalene and some of Jesus' women disciples were present at the cross and were the first to see the empty tomb. We do not, however, have much that describes Mary's personality or her relationship with Jesus. She is devoted to him, that much is clear, and John's Gospel fills out the picture of Mary Magdalene and her love for Jesus.

John's Gospel recounts that Mary was at the foot of the cross, and among the first to see the empty tomb and report it to Peter and the others. In this, he merely retells the tradition of the synoptics. It is only later that we get a fuller description of an encounter between Mary and the risen Jesus.

John presents Mary as very concerned about the body of Jesus. At this point in the story, she is focused on the physical presence of Jesus. She does not seem to remember Jesus' prediction of the resurrection; she simply presumes that the body of Jesus has been stolen or moved. Her desire is to honor Jesus' body by making sure it is safe and properly prepared for burial. So she returns to the tomb, weeping. This whole affair of

Jesus' rejection and death has been heart wrenching, but now to lose his body is almost too much for her to bear. Once again, Mary peers into the tomb, but this time she sees two angels who ask, "Woman, why are you weeping?" (John 20:13). Turning away from the tomb, she sees Jesus, but does not recognize him.

This lack of recognition is a theme in gospel appearance stories. It is a way of proclaiming that Jesus has changed. The resurrection is not simply a resuscitation of the dead body of Jesus. No, the risen Christ is the firstborn of a new reality. The same Jesus who walked the dusty roads of Palestine is now the glorified risen Lord, a truth so new that, at first, even his closest companions fail to recognize him (see Luke 24:13–35).

Jesus also asks Mary why she cries, and for whom she is looking. Mary, still focused on the physical absence of Jesus' body, can not see who it is who asks this question of her—perhaps, she thinks, he is the very one who has removed Jesus' body. But then Jesus calls her name, "Mary." At the sound of her name, Mary turns again. This time, however, she does not move, since she is already facing Jesus. She turns spiritually, in her heart, as she recognizes his voice and acknowledges his presence.[4]

Jesus calls her name. Like the Good Shepherd whose sheep know and heed his voice, Jesus breaks through Mary's grief and preoccupation by uttering one word—her name. Jesus says "Mary," as he must have said it many times before, for the new reality of the resurrection is not a break with the past, but one that carries it to a new level. Jesus calls Mary's name and invites her to enter into the new existence. Now she is summoned to look beyond the mere physical reality of Jesus' life. Previously she had taken care of Jesus' physical needs by providing for him out of her means. She came to the tomb to continue that care, but now is confronted with the new existence of Jesus that goes beyond the physical; Mary is called to see and understand the new relationship that resurrection makes possible.

Mary sees Jesus but does not yet fully grasp the difference. She calls him *Rabboni,* which means "my teacher." It is a familiar, intimate title, filled with respect. "My teacher" portrays the relationship which Mary and Jesus shared: he is not merely *a* teacher; he is not even *the* teacher. Mary calls him *my* teacher. In many ways, Mary parallels the Beloved Disciple as one of Jesus' favorites. She is loyal, dedicated, and attached to Jesus through a bond of love. She reaches out to embrace Jesus. Having once lost him, she seeks to hold on to him so that he will not, or perhaps cannot, get away. She is still seeing only the physical reality of Jesus' presence.

"Do not hold on to me," Jesus says in John 20:17. He is not really telling her not to touch him, but challenging her to let go of past perceptions. Now that she has "seen" him, Mary must "understand" him. Jesus' presence to Mary Magdalene is no longer limited to the physical person she once provided for and took care of. The love she bears for Jesus must rise to a higher level, not bound by place and time. It is the love that never ends (see 1 Cor 13:8). Once Mary understands this important lesson, she is sent to spread the good news to the community of Jesus' followers. She is the "apostle to the Apostles" (Rabanus Maurus † 856).[5] Mary of Magdala has been Jesus' companion and disciple, now she is his witness. We can tell of her conversion, her turning around, by her actions: she leaves the tomb and runs to the disciples. We can tell of her understanding of who Jesus is by her words: "I have seen the Lord" (John 20:18). She does not say, "I have seen my Teacher," because now she comprehends that he is more than teacher, he is the Lord whose love has conquered even death.

From these brief passages in the gospels, what can we say about the relationship between Jesus and Mary Magdalene?

What does their love for one another say to us about ourselves? Mary of Magdala's relationship with Jesus was intensely personal. That Luke refers to her cure from "seven demons" shows that her malady was serious and prolonged. We do not know the nature of it, but whether it was physical or emotional, her cure by Jesus did more for her than bring her relief from suffering. Mary's cure brought about her call to follow Jesus. It was unusual for a woman in first century Palestine to follow an itinerant preacher. The fact that Mary and other women did follow Jesus may have raised a few eyebrows in the establishment, but Mary and her companions felt that it was worth the risk. Yet for Mary, and those men and women who, like her, had experienced firsthand the healing power of Jesus' love, there was no other way to respond than to follow. Their loyalty was part of their response of love to the Lord. Perhaps because following Jesus at all was risky, the women in Jesus' company were more prepared to follow all the way to the cross. We can not say that Mary loved Jesus more than Peter or James or Thomas, but certainly her devotion to him gave her the strength of will not only to stand at the foot of the cross, but to be concerned about the final disposition of his body for burial.

This love is the love of loyalty and devotion. It is love that is willing to take risks for the sake of the beloved. It allows someone to stand by a friend who is in trouble, even if such loyalty might cause more trouble. Jesus' presence to Mary was a healing presence. True love brings healing. It looks beyond problems, or maybe even within the problem, and sees the potential of the whole person. Mary's commitment to Jesus was born of gratitude. Gratitude is a special grace that inspires friends to be there for each other, not in the sense of payback or obligation, but because of the bond of love that has been forged through tribulations. We are grateful for the love of our friends, and so we show our appreciation for that gift by the integrity of our own friendship.

Mary's love and gratitude led her to the cross of Jesus. As she had taken care of him in life, she was willing to take care of him in death. Yet she was also called to experience the love of Jesus in a more profound and intimate way. During Jesus' earthly life, Mary Magdalene had been concerned with his physical person. Now she was summoned to an intimacy of spirit that went beyond the physical. As she was invited to resurrection faith, she was also invited to resurrection love.

Resurrection love might be called a higher form of love, or at least a more profound love. Certainly, it characterized the love that led Mary Magdalene and all of Jesus' disciples to form the community we call the church. Luke in the Acts of the Apostles best describes the ideal of this love. The fellowship gathered in Jesus' name took care of each other, supported each other, and assembled in prayer as a family in order to manifest their love for Jesus. Mary ran back to tell Jesus' followers, "I have seen the Lord," not merely because he told her to, but because she already shared in the love of the community still only in its infancy.

This spiritual love that binds a community together also has its more personal side. Mary still shares a particular relationship with the Lord, but not one based on physical presence. She can no longer cling to Jesus, but in letting go, she does not lose him either. This love is experienced even in absence. It is often a difficult love. Those who have lost a loved one through death experience this kind of love. It is a love of mind and heart and memory. It is often a bittersweet love because the absence of the beloved is keenly felt. Yet, the true love of spouse, parents, family, and friends can never be taken away. Often a memory or place can make us feel the presence of a dead loved one, or in a time of difficulty and crisis, we know that the same absent friend or spouse is with us. This is not a feeling or apparition; it is a conviction. Even in death, a loved one can bring out the best in us. This experience is the basis for the church's teaching on the Communion of Saints; we are still connected with those who have gone before us. Our departed loved ones still touch our lives and this connection can only be expressed in the words of love. Further, the love we bear toward one another, as family, friends and church, is a sign of our love for a departed loved one. We keep alive our love for them when we love others. Such is resurrection love.

The love between Jesus and Mary of Magdala was a healing, redeeming love. It forged a bond between them that even death could not break. Such a love is a graced experience that connects people, families, and communities together. It is a love that goes beyond the physical to the spiritual. It pierces into the depths of our hearts. This love draws us out of ourselves, and into relationships that have no end because they are based in that living love that is Christ, the risen Lord.

Reflection Questions

1. What do the gospels say about Mary of Magdala? How is this picture different from traditional understandings?
2. How does "resurrection faith" change Mary's relationship to Jesus?
3. What does it mean to have "resurrection love" in your life?

Notes

1. The history of devotion and thought about Mary Magdalene is beyond the scope of this work. For a great summary of scriptural, Apocryphal, and traditional material about her, see Mary R. Thompson, S.S.M.N. *Mary*

Magdalene Apostle and Leader. New York: Paulist Press, 1995.

2. Ardy Evenson, "Mary of Magdala," *The Bible Today* 27: 4 July, 1989, p. 221.
3. Thompson, pp. 3–9.
4. Thompson, pp. 74–75.
5. Rabanus Maurus. *De vita beatae Mariae Magdelenae*, 27, PL 112, 1474.

CHAPTER THIRTEEN

Jesus and Peter

"Simon, do you love me?"

As we have seen, Jesus had the ability to form close ties of love and friendship with people that called them to a higher, more intimate love. The gospels tell us that even among his immediate disciples, yes, even within the Twelve, there were special friends. Peter, James, and John seem to have had a deeper relationship with the Lord than the others. They were present at events witnessed by no one else, such as the raising of Jairus' daughter (Luke 8:51), and the transfiguration (Matt 17:1). These three stayed close to Jesus in the Garden of Gethsemane (Mark 14:33). Even within this close circle of friends, one stands out in a unique way as a special person in Jesus' life. Simon Peter is mentioned over and over as Jesus' special friend.

The New Testament mentions Peter more than it mentions any other of Jesus' followers. From the gospel passages in both the Synoptics and John, Peter's character comes through in his words and his actions. After Jesus, he is the most developed personality in the gospels, from a literary point of view. He comes down to us as a headstrong, impetuous, and impulsive man. He was quick to speak, even sometimes speaking before he thought things through. He was the acknowledged spokesperson for the Twelve (maybe because no one else could

get a word in). By trade, he was a fisherman; by nature, a
leader. He and his brother Andrew were from Bethsaida but
had moved to Capernaum, which was also the base of Jesus'
Galilean ministry. John's Gospel portrays Peter as a disciple of
John the Baptist before John sent him to follow Jesus.[1]

Peter also had his weaknesses. His natural tendency to
speak out caused him to bluster. Like the other disciples, he
often misunderstood Jesus, and even tried to steer Jesus away
from the path the Lord had chosen. We are all familiar with
Peter's denials of Christ on the night before the crucifixion, an
incident recounted in all four gospels. Even Simon's nickname,
Peter (which means *rock*), implies a certain stubbornness and
immaturity in Peter's character.

Yet, Jesus had a special friendship with Simon Peter. Christ
saw something in him that allowed him to put his faith in Peter.
Jesus' friendship with him challenged Peter to stretch himself,
to become a better person, and to come to know Jesus' love in
a unique way. Two passages from the gospels stand out as
examples of the relationship between Peter and the Lord. Both
passages surround the story of the miraculous catch of fish.
One version, Luke 5:1–11, takes place at the beginning of Jesus'
ministry, and his relationship with Peter; the other account,
John 21:1–19, happens after the resurrection. Both passages
show how Jesus' love for Peter called Peter to be more than he
thought he could be.

The two stories of the miraculous catch of fish have much
in common. Scholars generally believe that they are independent interpretations of one event. Luke and John adapted this
tradition about an extraordinary catch of fish to suit their own
theological purposes in putting forth the gospel message. Most
scholars believe that the original story was of a post-resurrection appearance of Jesus to Peter that Luke has placed in the
beginning of the Lord's public ministry to highlight Peter's call.

The two main characters in both accounts are Jesus and Peter, and the story gives us a singular glimpse into the relationship between Jesus called Christ and Simon called Peter.

First, let us look at elements that are common to both versions of the story. Both envision a long night of fishing that was unsuccessful. By Jesus' invitation, the disciples cast their nets one more time, and receive for their efforts a fantastic reward. In both stories, the condition of the nets is noted (though it is different in the two accounts, Luke saying that it was near breaking, and John maintaining that it was full, but not broken). Luke and John both highlight Peter's reaction to this turn of events.

The stories have their differences as well. The list of who accompanies Peter in the boat is different. In Luke, Jesus is in the boat, too, while John has him on the shore. As noted earlier, Luke has this episode occur at the beginning of the Galilean ministry, while John has it happen after the resurrection. In both versions, however, Peter is invited to take on a pastoral ministry at the story's end.[2]

Luke indicates that Peter was already a disciple of sorts. Earlier in the gospel (Luke 4:38–39) Jesus had healed Peter's mother-in-law. Jesus chose to sit in Simon Peter's boat to address the crowd on the lakeshore (5:3), after which, Jesus instructed Peter to put out to sea again in search of fish. Peter, the professional fishermen, is skeptical, but follows the Lord's directions. The result is so large a catch of fish that Simon must call to his partners (James and John, Zebedee's sons) to help haul the nets (which are breaking) ashore.

The reaction of all the disciples is amazement, but Peter's response is unique. He falls on his knees at Jesus' feet (not an easy task in a fishing boat), and says, "Go away from me, Lord, for I am a sinful man" (5:8). This incident has caused Peter to have an insight into Jesus' person that has shaken him to the core. Touched by the power of Jesus' words and actions, Peter realizes that Jesus is more than a simple itinerant rabbi with a new hook on the old religion. The personality of Jesus brings Peter to a self-realization. He is faced with a truth about himself. He is a sinner in the presence of goodness. He sees himself in all his bluster and faults, and he shies away, not because he is unwilling to change, but because he is afraid that he cannot. Remember, Peter is a professional fisherman, he knows this lake and what it is capable of producing, and this catch shows him that Jesus has power over the forces of nature. This power acts as a mirror into Simon's own soul, and he is over-awed. "Leave me," he says, "I am unable to rise to the task of following you."

Jesus' response is not surprising. He does now to Peter what he does so often in the gospels: he speaks a healing word. "Do not be afraid." Jesus' love cuts through Peter's self-doubt. "Fear not," he tells him, "I know who you are and what you are. I have always known, and yet I love you still." Jesus sees past the hesitancy, the sinfulness, the bluster, and the weakness that make up Peter's personality. His love sees Peter's potential, not just what he is, but what he *can be*. "Do not be afraid." Peter may have some growing up to do, but he will not be alone. Jesus' love will change him, and help him to become more than he ever thought he could be. "From now on, you will be catching people" (Luke 5:10).

And so Peter is called to ministry. He is not just to be a follower of Jesus—one who merely listens to his teachings. Peter is called to use his gifts and talents to bring people into the community of believers. He will leave behind the nets and boats of his trade, the familiar life of a fisherman, and strike out on the mission with Jesus. Perhaps this realization is part of Peter's hesitation in following Jesus. But once he is called, Peter responds: "He left everything and followed him" (5:11).

Peter followed. From town to town in Galilee, through the Decapolis and down into Judea and Jerusalem, he followed.

With enthusiasm he went on his first preaching mission (Luke 9:1–6; Matt 10:5–15). Sometimes he did not understand Jesus (Matt 16:22–23; Mark 8:32–33), and still he followed. He followed to the Last Supper, protesting his willingness to follow Jesus to prison and death (Luke 22:33). Though sleepy, he went with Jesus to the Garden of Gethsemane (Matt 26:36ff; Mark 14:32ff; Luke 22:39ff). When all the other disciples had fled in terror after Jesus' arrest, only Peter and the Beloved Disciple still followed, even into the courtyard of the high priest (John 18:15–18). Yes, Peter followed Jesus even when the rest of the Twelve had abandoned him, afraid to be known as Jesus' companions. Peter did follow Jesus farther than the others, but then his courage failed. The sinfulness and unworthiness that he felt kneeling in the boat in Galilee flooded in upon him, and Peter denied Jesus. To save his own skin, three times Peter vehemently denied the Lord he had followed so long and so well. All four gospels recount it, not sparing Peter, nor trying in any way to soften the betrayal. It is not as if there was any doubt that Peter loved Jesus. In fact, Peter's love for Jesus made his denials even worse. When push came to shove, when Jesus needed Peter the most, Peter could not find the courage to follow.

We can only imagine the feelings Peter experienced on Good Friday morning. He failed his friend. Maybe more painful than even Jesus' death was the fact that Peter had denied him. The other disciples had merely run away as cowards, but Peter had sunk lower. He had been given the opportunity to prove his love for the Lord, to stand beside him in his hour of need, yet fear had taken over and Peter betrayed Jesus' friendship, and when the rooster crowed, "he went out and wept bitterly" (Luke 22:62).

Through Friday and Saturday, Peter mourned Jesus and cursed himself for his weakness. Slowly, the community of

Jesus' followers reformed. They had nowhere else to go, and without the Master, did not know what to do. Overwhelmed with sadness, fear, and guilt, they sat in the upper room and waited. For what? They probably did not know themselves. Then came Sunday morning and the impossible news from Mary Magdalene and the women who had gone to the tomb. It was empty! "I have seen the Lord!" says Mary. And then the wonderful events of Easter night happened. The Lord stands in their midst. "Peace be with you" (John 20:1), he says, and "Receive the Holy Spirit" (John 20:22). The Lord is risen, and he renews the call to follow him.

And what is Simon Peter's response to all of these amazing events? "I am going fishing," he declares (John 21:3). So we come back to the starting point, in a fishing boat on the lake, and John's account of the miraculous catch of fish. Many scholars argue that this scene comes from an independent "first contact" resurrection account connected with a post-resurrection meal story. They maintain that Peter's desire to go fishing is incompatible with previous appearance accounts. Would Peter have gone back to Galilee and returned to fishing if he had witnessed the risen Christ on Easter night? I do not think that it is out of the question.

Peter is overwhelmed by the events of the Passion. Jesus' death, combined with his own personal failures as a friend, have left him wounded and uncertain. His bluster is gone, and his conscience is tormented. The resurrection, on a merely human level, *increased* rather than *decreased*, his self-doubt. So his response, "I am going fishing," is entirely understandable. He returns to familiar territory. Sensing his failure as a "people-catcher," he goes back to catching fish. Yet, he is still a leader, since some of the other disciples join him in this "safe" fishing venture. Back to the familiar and routine they go, and spend a frustrating night of fruitless labor.

"Just after daybreak," we are told, "Jesus stood on the beach" (John 21:4). A new day dawns, and with it, new hope. Following the motif of similar "resurrection appearances," the disciples do not recognize Jesus at first. There is something so different about him that even his closest friends cannot discern who he is. Jesus acts in familiar form, however, and he calls out to the weary fishermen:

> Cast the net to the right side of the boat, and you will find some [fish]. (John 21:6)

Almost inexplicably, the fishermen follow this stranger's instructions. Maybe he sees something from the shore that they cannot. Maybe there is just something about his personality, his tone of voice, his presence, that moves them to obey. So they cast their nets, and are rewarded. They catch so many fish that they find it hard to haul it in—it is a miracle! Where once there were no fish, now there are more than they can handle. One of those in the boat is the Beloved Disciple. He puts two and two together and realizes who this stranger is. It can be none other than Jesus. That the Beloved Disciple recognizes Jesus first is a theme of John's Gospel that we will examine in the next chapter. What is important here is that he tells Simon Peter, "It is the Lord!" (John 21:7).

Peter's reaction is characteristic of him. He wraps his cloak about himself and jumps into the water. The impetuous, impulsive Peter is back. His love and excitement for Jesus overcomes his self-doubt. It is obvious that Jesus has come looking for him, so he jumps into the water, swimming, wading, and splashing toward the Lord. Is this a second chance he is getting? Peter does not seem to care; he only wants to be near the Lord. He wants to listen once again to his words, and sit at the feet of the Master. The power of Jesus over nature has a reverse effect on Peter this time. Instead of asking Jesus to leave, it gives Peter the confidence to stay.

The rest of the disciples come ashore and share a meal with Jesus (see also Luke 24:30 and 24:41–43). After breakfast, Peter and Jesus have a dialogue that helps complete our picture of their friendship. Apropos of nothing, it seems, Jesus asks Peter, "Simon, son of John, do you love me more than these?" (John 21:15). This question becomes the starting point of the discussion, not just about Peter's love, but also about the "these" to which Jesus refers. Is Jesus talking about the other disciples? If so, it would be a very insulting question to ask, with all of them sitting around listening. Would they not also protest their love for the Lord? Would Jesus set up this kind of competition between his followers? It does not seem character-istic of the Johannine Jesus to do so.

Remember that Peter has returned to his former lifestyle, even if just for a day. In Luke, this miraculous catch of fish has motivated Peter to follow Jesus; he "left everything and fol-lowed him" (Luke 5:11). Now Jesus asks once again that Peter be his disciple. "Do you love me more than these?" refers to the boat, the nets, and the sea, which are the familiar things of Peter's life that he will now have to leave behind entirely. Following Jesus has a cost, and Jesus wants to know if Simon is willing to pay it. "Do you love me more than your livelihood and lifestyle?" Peter responds, "Yes, Lord; you know that I love you" (21:15). Despite everything that has gone before—failure, backsliding, doubt, and fear—Peter proclaims his love for Jesus, and once again Jesus calls Peter to a pastoral mission. "Feed my lambs." How can Peter show his love for the Lord? He can take care of that which belongs to Jesus.

The Lord then asks a second time, "Simon, son of John, do you love me?" (21:16), and Peter answers, "Yes Lord, you know that I love you." Again the response comes, "Tend my sheep." Finally, for a third time, Jesus asks the same question, yet not quite the same. The first two times Jesus used the Greek word *agapē* (i.e., God-like love), and Peter responded with the Greek word *phileō* (i.e., brotherly or familial love). This third time, however, Jesus uses the term *phileō*, and Peter responds in kind. Jesus called Peter to a higher form of love, but met Peter at the level of his ability. One day Peter would love Jesus with *agapē* (see John 21:18–19), the selfless, self-sacrificing love. For now, it is enough that Peter loves Jesus as much as he is able.

Peter's final response makes it clear: "Lord, you know everything; you know that I love you" (21:17). Peter is saying, "Lord, you know me, and everything about me. You know my strength, my weakness, my faults, and yes, even my sins. You know my heart, too, and my heart belongs to you. I do love you." In response, Jesus says one last time, "Feed my sheep."

What can we say about this love of Peter and Jesus for one another, and what does it tell us of our own experience of love? The friendship Jesus and Simon Peter enjoyed was a special friendship, the kind that is rare. Most of us can say that we have many friends, but we are blessed when we know the love of a special friend, whose very life is entwined with ours in an often undefinable way. What do we see in this special friend, and what qualities draw us together? We are often at a loss to put it into words. What did Jesus see in Peter, the impetuous and brash fisherman of Galilee? Jesus saw more in Peter than Peter ever saw in himself. Love can do that. It can look beyond the surface and see the potential. It encourages growth and challenges us to reach for more, and yet accepts us as we are.

Further, this special friendship is a healing, reconciling friendship. Jesus' love healed Peter's doubts and failures. Friends provide safe places for one another; places where they can be vulnerable. Places where they can "go fishing," but are ultimately pulled back into life. The healing comes when we look into the eyes of a friend and see ourselves as they see us—as Jesus saw Peter, his friend. Friends provide confidence and hope.

This unique friendship is a key that unlocks our own ability to love. It calls for a return. We find each other through this love which calls us out of ourselves, and makes us more fully into who we want to be. It is a quality of our relationship to Jesus as Christians, and it is also the age-old experience of friends and loved ones in life. We answer the question, "Do you love me?" by our words and actions, our loyalty, and our forgiveness. We grow into more loving people by the friendship of those who see us as loveworthy.

Reflection Questions

1. How does Peter's relationship to Jesus change him? What does having a relationship with Jesus do for us?
2. What difficulties do we face when following Jesus? What ways can we deny him with our words and deeds?
3. What is the connection between Peter's love for Jesus and the pastoral ministry entrusted to him by Jesus? What does this connection say about us?

Notes

1. For a picture of Peter's role in the Scriptures, see: Raymond E. Brown, S.S., Karl P. Donfried and John Reumann, eds. *Peter in the New Testament,* New York: Paulist Press, 1973.
2. John Amedee Bailey. *The Traditions Common to the Gospels of Luke and John.* Supplements to the Novum Testamentum, Vol. VII. Leiden: E. J. Brill, 1963, pp. 12–17.

CHAPTER FOURTEEN

The Beloved Disciple

The disciple whom Jesus loved.

At the end of the dialogue between Jesus and Peter in John 21, a brief appendix is included concerning the enigmatic figure known as "the Beloved Disciple." It pertains to a tradition about this unnamed follower of Jesus that he would not die before the Second Coming. He did die, however, and the final editor of John's Gospel wanted to set the record straight. Jesus did not tell Peter that this disciple would not die, but that it was none of Peter's concern; Peter was to follow Jesus even if it meant martyrdom. What others did, or where their paths led, was not to affect Peter's mission to "feed my sheep."

The Gospel of John goes on to say, by way of conclusion:

This is the disciple who is testifying to these things and has written them, and we know that his testimony is true. (John 21:24)

Thus, it is this "disciple whom Jesus loved" who has brought us the unique witness of the Fourth Gospel. But who was he, and what was his relationship to Jesus? What can we learn from the Beloved Disciple about love and about *our* relationship to the Lord?

Biblical scholars and commentators have filled pages upon pages trying to identify the Beloved Disciple and his role in the composition of the gospel we call "John."[1] Ireneaus, in the late second century, identified the Beloved Disciple with John, the son of Zebedee, thus making the author of the gospel an apostle and follower of Jesus from the beginning of the Lord's ministry. This designation has been popular throughout the centuries, but has fallen into disfavor in recent scholarship. First of all, the gospel itself never so identifies its author, nor does it refer to the disciple as an apostle. We know from all the gospels that Jesus had many close followers apart from the Twelve. It is theorized that one of these was the founder of a tradition (most probably oral in nature) that emphasized close personal relationship with Jesus, and the role of the Paraclete or Holy Spirit in holding the community together. This community produced a certain school of thought about the life and meaning of Jesus that preserved the witness of this disciple in the New Testament writings attributed to John (i.e., the gospel and three letters, as well as the Book of Revelation). This disciple was a revered figure in this community, and was the eyewitness upon which the gospel was based. While this disciple did not "write" the gospel as we know it, he is the "authority" for its vision and theology. In this sense, he is the author. His relationship with Jesus was intensely personal, and so he was designated "the disciple whom Jesus loved."[2]

It is this relationship we wish to examine. What qualities in this disciple caused him to be so "beloved?" His first appearance in the gospel is at the Last Supper, what Jesus describes as his "hour" (John 13), but already he was part of Jesus' band of followers. He sits at the place of honor at the meal, and shows a particular intimacy with Jesus in conversation (John 13:22–26). Later, it is said that he was known to the high priest (John 18:15), so he must have had connections with the Jerusalem establishment. He is the only male disciple of Jesus to follow all the way to the cross, where he is given responsibility for the mother of the Lord. He runs with Peter to see the empty tomb (John 20:3–10), and is the first to recognize the risen Jesus by the lakeside in John 21. In all these stories, we catch only glimpses of him; he remains mysterious and almost anonymous. What is known and emphasized about him is that he loved Jesus and that Jesus loved him. Love, of course, is the point. It is what makes this disciple of Jesus the hero of this so-called Johanine Community. He became the symbolic measuring stick for all of Jesus' followers, even Simon Peter. What is the disciple supposed to do? Follow Jesus. How is the disciple supposed to follow? By loving Jesus. In this way the unnamed disciple becomes the representative of *all* disciples. Who is the Beloved Disciple? We all are. How do we become the Beloved Disciple? By loving Jesus. How is this love expressed? When we love one another as Jesus loves us. This love is the other side of the coin, "God is love."

The Beloved Disciple, then, shows us how to be disciples ourselves. To follow Jesus is to be one with him in love. Peter had to learn this truth so that he could take on the pastoral ministry of tending the Lord's flock. The Beloved Disciple, however, seems to have perceived this truth from the beginning. He leads the way, in the Fourth Gospel, in love, faith, and response to the Lord. Present for the last discourse of Jesus at the Last Supper (John 14–17), the Beloved Disciple has heard the new commandment:

> Love one another. Just as I have loved you, you also should love one another. By this everyone will know that you are my disciples, if you have love for one another. (John 14:34)

This love characterizes the Beloved Disciple. This love characterizes the community of disciples; this love should characterize us. How well we live out this commandment is how well we show our love for Jesus. This reality brings us back to the starting point of our exploration—abiding in God's love. The Beloved Disciple dwelt in the love of the Lord. He was not content merely to lean upon the Lord's heart at the Last Supper; he took the risk to follow Jesus to the cross. In taking responsibility for the mother of Jesus, he, too, took on a pastoral responsibility. Jesus' mother was a widow, and widows were one of the most powerless groups in society. She, also, is a symbolic figure—she represents the family of Jesus, which is the community of believers. So love for Jesus reaches out to embrace the whole church, especially the poor and powerless. If we are also "Beloved Disciples," then this same care is our way of loving.

Having a relationship with Jesus Christ is what it means to be Christian; it's so simple, and yet sometimes we can forget this important truth. It is more than faith in Jesus; it is more than believing in the saving actions of Jesus' life, death, and resurrection. Being Christian is more than respect for Jesus' teachings and his worldview. It is about having a relationship with him. For the Christian, the personal connection with the Lord Jesus is the whole point of the love story that began with Creation. The incarnation of Jesus is what makes sense out of the entire story we have experienced in this book. It is why the creation of man and woman "in the image and likeness of God" (Gen 1:27) is the culmination of God's creative love. Humanity's creation in the image of God comes to its fullest expression in the person of Jesus, fully divine and fully human. Jesus defines what it means to be human. He is at once the starting point and the goal of all creation—that we might unite ourselves with God through Christ. As St. Paul says:

> He is the image of the invisible God, the firstborn of all creation; for in him all things in heaven and on earth

were created...all things have been created through him and for him. (Col 1:15–16)

Abiding in love comes to a new and intimate meaning when we strive to live as Jesus did. What made the Beloved Disciple beloved was that he understood this truth: it is the basis for his whole testimony to Jesus in the gospel and the letters. We become the "Beloved Disciple" ourselves when we take this reality to heart and abide in God's love.

How does this love play itself out in our lives? It is intensely practical. We are given the opportunities of being Beloved Disciples every day, and every day we succeed or fail in the measure that we love. It begins in our family. Do we take the time and effort to cherish and respect those individuals who are our own flesh and blood? Or is our family life more like Jacob's, filled with deceit, rivalry, and discord? Chances are that we can answer yes to both questions. We all play a part in our family relationships, for good and for bad, and even if we are not the cause of the friction or distress, we can choose not to add to it. While loving responses may be tough, and we may have to clearly state and preserve our boundaries when it comes to our familial relationships, we still have the ability to act in loving ways to our brothers and sisters, parents and children.

Even in Jacob's family, Joseph was able to forgive and bring reconciliation to his brothers. He did not ignore their responsibility for what happened, but he did see how good things came of it. Instead of nursing a grudge for years, Joseph was able to let go of past hurts, overcome his resentment, and bring peace to his family. Somewhere, he too learned about love, and expressed it in forgiveness and acceptance.

The decision to be a loving person—to abide in love—directs the course of our human relationships. Like Ruth and Boaz, people of substance find one another. The loving disciple has values and convictions that not only define who he or she is, but serve to attract like-valued people into his or her life. The loving and self-sacrificing Ruth is met at her level by the generous and respectful Boaz, and their love moves forth God's plan of salvation as they become the ancestors of David and Jesus. The decisions we make in everyday life about what is important to us place us within this same plan of salvation.

Similarly, through loyalty and devotion, we form friendships that mirror the faithful care of our God. David and Jonathan personify that friendship. It is friendship that stands the test of time and adversity. Their love called forth the best in their personalities, and David is a better person for having known Jonathan. We, too, journey through life, not alone, but in the company of friends. How do we choose them? How do we treat them? We can inspire the best in them while rising to the best in ourselves, or we can take advantage of their friendship to advance our own ambition, and ultimately lose their love. The choice is ours, and yet, how much more we can discover about the love of God through the open and honest love of our friends. How much we can *see* and *be* Christ's presence to one another through friendships that promote faithfulness, strength of character, and the ability to see good in each other.

Sometimes, however, our love is challenged, and betrayal repays our loyalty. We saw how Hosea the prophet reacted to the devastation of his wife Gomer's infidelity. Hosea struggled to forgive, but also dealt with feelings of anger, hurt, and frustration. While he believed in the importance of faithfulness on his own part, he also knew the struggle and brokenness that makes such faithfulness difficult. Often our damaged relationships have no solution. We grapple to maintain our values when everything around us fights against them. As the Beloved Disciple stood beneath the cross, and felt its despair, we too can bear the cross of hurt and disloyalty, and only hope to find the presence of God in our lives.

At other times, difficulties present themselves even before love has a chance to blossom. Certainly the history that Sarah brought to her relationship with Tobias was an obstacle to their love. Family history, past relationships, fears, and expectations can possess us and prevent us from taking the risk to love at all. Yet, faith in God and in another person brings healing, dismissing the demons of the past. We open our eyes to the possibilities love can offer. Such faith allowed Tobias and Sarah to find each other. Such faith gives us strength to love as well.

Abiding in love, and living as beloved disciples, can touch every area of our lives. Our sexuality itself is a sign of the goodness of God. We relate to one another in loving ways, and form that special bond of friendship we call married love. God is present in our loving, in the delight of lovers, and in the play of erotic love between them. This love finds its source in commitment. The God who created us as male and female, and who enables us to express our love through our sexuality, brings to completion in us the mandate to be fruitful, and shows us how intimate our love with God can be. Marriage partners find Christ in each other, and know in the depths of their relationships, in both good and bad times, what it means to abide in love.

As love requires commitment, it is also a choice, or better, a series of choices, as we saw in the relationship of Joseph toward Mary and Jesus. Some choices are difficult to make, but love enables and strengthens. Oftentimes, love requires us to take a risk by having faith in another person. Joseph trusted his God and the message and mission given to him. He also trusted in Mary and her role in God's plan. His trust gave him the power to love.

Trust can be a difficult commodity, often lacking in our world. Yet, without it, we can never form the bonds that allow true love to flourish. For Joseph it began with his faith that God's word was true, and having found God to be trustworthy, he was able to trust Mary, to take Jesus as his own, and provide for him and his mother. Love requires this trust, and the decisions we make based on it help us to grow in the love of God and each other.

So, too, Mary trusted and acted in loving ways. She trusted that God's word to her was true, and she trusted in Joseph's strength of character to support and believe her. She translated that trust into loving concern for Elizabeth, and tender care for the infant Jesus. She knew and experienced how love turns things around, and makes the impossible possible. In turn, through love, Mary herself became a "beloved disciple" who followed Jesus to the cross, and to resurrection. Thus Mary, mother, wife, and disciple, becomes the model for all Christian disciples.

Love calls us to become our better selves. In the presence of a loved one, we drop our defenses and become our true selves. We are able to transcend that which keeps us down and imprisons us within our own loneliness. Mary Magdalene, healed of sin and sickness, went on to become one of Jesus' most loyal followers. She followed even to the cross, and beyond. Love does that for us. We join our lives to the beloved person, and become willing to share with them the ups and downs of life. We see this love in someone's devotion toward a sick spouse, or in the way that friends stand by each other in times of testing and trial. It is through these difficult times that love raises us up in hope. Love enabled Mary to recognize the risen Jesus when he called her name. Resurrection is an experience of love—love that cannot die.

As we have seen, love brings with it forgiveness, acceptance, and challenge. Sometimes this love can be overwhelming. Faced with such love, Simon Peter balked at following Jesus.

Love can be frightening. Love can also be inviting. Jesus' call broke through Peter's hesitation, and even when Peter had betrayed Jesus' love, this loving call brought Peter not only forgiveness, but renewed strength and courage. True love builds up, gives confidence, and inspires trust. As we have seen, love is fruitful in many ways. As Peter became fruitful through the pastoral ministry that Jesus entrusted to him, we, too, become fruitful by growing into the challenge that love gives to us—a challenge to become more than we thought we could.

So, as Beloved Disciples, as loving beings created in the image and likeness of God, we live our call by the way we love. In our very human experiences we create a dwelling place of love. In both the triumphs and the hurts of our human loving, we experience the loving God. Love cannot but tell us of God. Love can do nothing apart from God, and love draws us into the mystery of God. That mystery is experienced in our lives by the mystery of love, by the relationships and friendships that bring us love and give us the opportunities to give love. We can only sum it up in the words:

God is love!

Reflection Questions

1. How does the Beloved Disciple model love for us in the Gospel of John?
2. What is the difference between faith in Jesus and love for Jesus? How does the latter effect the former?
3. What qualities of the Beloved Disciple have we seen in the biblical characters examined throughout this book?

Notes

1. The various theories concerning the Beloved Disciple can be summarized by the following: Raymond E. Brown, S.S. *The Gospel According to John*. Anchor Bible, Garden City: Doubleday & Company, 1966; Martin Hengel, *The Johanine Question;* Trans. John Bowden, Philadelphia: Trinity Press International, 1989; Francis J. Moloney, S.D.B. *The Gospel of John*. Sacra Pagina. Ed. Daniel Harrington, S.J., Collegeville: The Liturgical Press, 1998.
2. Raymond E. Brown, S.S. *The Community of the Beloved Disciple,* New York: Paulist Press, 1979, pp. 25–34.